Light Your Fire

Light Your Fire

How Leveraging Strengths
Will Inspire You and Your Team
Members toward Skyrocketing Success!

Keith Baldwin

Published by
RockStar Publishing House
32129 Lindero Canyon Road, Suite 205
Westlake Village, CA 91361
www.rockstarpublishinghouse.com

Manufactured in the United States of America,
or in the United Kingdom when distributed elsewhere.

Baldwin, Keith
Light Your Fire: How leveraging strengths will inspire
you and your team members towards skyrocketing success
   ISBN:
   Paperback: 9781937506971
   eBook: 9781937506988

Cover design by: Joe Potter

Interior design: Scribe Inc.

Author's URL: www.baldwinsuccesscoaching.com

Acknowledgments

My writing professor, Jane Evanson, once told me, "No one writes a book by themselves." That is certainly true in this case! This book would not have been possible without the guidance, support, and work of many people. After Jane sparked my initial desire to write a book came Craig Duswalt, creator of the RockStar System for Success, who encourages all entrepreneurs to write a book in 30 days. His system, and my wife's creative way of using it, made the project less overwhelming and very doable.

Thank you to Jacob Graham who questioned and then patiently listened to hours and hours of my ideas on these concepts. Those conversations formed the foundation of this book.

Thank you to all my clients for being open to exploring all these ideas with your teams and businesses. Your dedication to your clients, teams, and future inspires me. Special thanks to Todd Jackson and Al Bowler, the first entrepreneurs to ask me "How could your coaching help me with my teams and business?"

It's so cool to be part of a worldwide strengths movement. Thank you to the people at Gallup headquarters for making my wife and I feel like family. Building a worldwide strengths community is not easy! Jim Collison is our "glue"—he ensures a continual stream of powerful strengths content in his role of Strengths Community Manager and producer of Gallup's "Called to Coach" and "Theme Thursday" webcasts, which can be found at www.coaching.gallup.com. Thank you, Jim!

Thank you to my fellow certified strengths coaches around the world— especially Johan Oosthuizen in South Africa!

It's hard to explain the power of a powerful mentor. Larry Broughton continues to help me believe in myself and always encourages me to step on a bigger platform. His continual transparency, vulnerability, and integrity encourage me to be the same—in pursuit of sharing all that I am and all that I know in the hopes it will someday serve others.

This book would not have happened without the patience, persistence, and dedication of my editor Danielle Lattuga (www.lattugacreative.com). Thank you for pushing me to keep moving forward, for taking my very rough ideas and turning them into something readable. This book wouldn't be here without you.

Thank you to Karen Strauss, publisher of RockStar Publishing House, for your guidance and consistent pressure to get this book done! You and Danielle made it easy.

And finally, thank you to my business partner and wife, Cindy Baldwin, who offered content for the Sales section and edited many drafts of this book to help clarify the ideas rattling around in my head. After being together more than 40 years, she can somehow read my mind. Scary!

For my wife, Cindy,
who believed in me before I believed in myself

Contents

Foreword   ix

Introduction   xiii

Section 1: Light Your Fire

1. Finding Inspiration in Your Business   3
2. The Sweet Spot: An Introduction to Strengths   5

Section 2: Lead from Strengths

3. The Spark of a Well-Rounded Team   11
4. The Business Success Wheel©: A Tool to Drive Success   15
5. Strengths-Based Business Leadership   19
6. Three Steps to Igniting Your Strengths   23
7. How Your Talents Become Strengths   25

Section 3: Build a 90-Day Game Plan

8. Three Steps to a Business Plan That Sees the Light of Day   31
9. Vision/Mission/Values   35
10. Objectives/Strategies/Tactics   43

Section 4: Focus Your Time

11. High-Leverage Activities Drive Results   59
12. The Four Hats of a Business Leader   63
13. The Distinction between Mentoring and Coaching   67
14. Feeding the Flame: Become a Talent Connoisseur   71

Section 5: Focus Your Team's Time

15. The Burn of the Production Curve   77
16. Fire Control: Attention to Daily Results   81
17. How Meetings Support Your Tactics . . . and Your Success!   85
18. The Traffic Light: Measuring Your Daily Success   89

Section 6: Engage Your Team

19.	Four Keys to Extraordinary Employee Performance	95
20.	Understanding Employee Engagement	99
21.	Strengths-Based Sales	103
22.	Why Building Trust Is Essential for Highly Engaged Teams	113
23.	Four Obstacles to a Truly Engaged Team	117

Conclusion	121
Book Resources	125
Bibliography	127

Foreword

Larry Broughton

What will happen when we think about what is right with people
rather than fixating on what is wrong with them?

DONALD O. CLIFTON

I love living a life of possibility, optimism, and inspiration. Combine those warm
fuzzies with knowledge, talent, and some rapid action, and I've suddenly got
rocket fuel for my ideas and daily intentions.

I've actively studied high-potential entrepreneurs, leaders, and achievers for
the past couple of decades and have found it heartbreaking to see many of them
fall short of their goals or actually quit just shy of their destiny due to frustration,
fatigue, and burnout. Do you ever wonder why that happens? Can you relate?

Imagine how different the world could become if we all started living and performing to our fullest potential. Sure, it's a great dream, but it's not likely to happen in our lifetimes. Thank God, however, there are sages and sculptors dedicated
to creating warriors out of mounds of clay in an effort to move the needle in that
direction. One such sage is the author of the book you hold in your hands, Keith
Baldwin. I appreciate his heart and his mission to make the world great by making
great leaders. If you know the history of leadership development and the peak potential movement, you know Keith's not the first with such a noble cause, but he
is one of the wisest, most selfless, and most effective coaches and mentors I know.

I've been blessed to have had several engaging conversations about human potential, strengths-based leadership, and elite team building with Keith over the past
several years. Although neither of us particularly like the truth of this, we're both
believers that reality is our friend. So here's a dose of reality every leader needs to
understand: employees don't quit their jobs; they quit their managers and leaders.
If you're the manager or leader of an organization, let that sink in for just a moment. The last time (and the time before that, and even the time before that) an
employee quit your organization, it's quite likely they quit *you*, not the *job*. Ouch!
Did that sting a little bit? Good. It hurts me every time it happens to me, and it
should be a solemn reminder of our moral obligation to develop great people.

The truth is, too often employees (or "team members" as we call them in our
organizations) quit because they're not receiving the professional development they
crave, and they're "asked" to work well outside their strengths—which makes work
an absolutely morale-busting daily grind. Have you ever reflected on how you'd

feel if every day you went to work, you had to spend 80-plus percent of your time doing things you don't enjoy, doing things you're not good at? Ugh! Welcome to the American workforce. Now play that movie forward a couple more minutes.

When an employee's life is a grind because he or she feels unfulfilled and unappreciated at work and worries that he or she may not be great at his or her job—how do you imagine he or she feels about himself or herself? The ugly truth is, he or she takes that burden home, and that disappointment creeps in to other areas of his or her life. As it turns out, these are major contributors to why people give up on all sorts of lofty goals and dreams. But let's flip that around for a second. Imagine if every member on your team were able to spend most of their time on projects and tasks they enjoyed doing and were good at . . . How would the tone and culture of your workplace change? If your organization is like most, sparks would fly: productivity, morale, retention, and profitability would skyrocket.

At the core of many great leaders throughout history is the concept of "servant leadership." When applied with conviction, this concept encourages leaders to lead by being of service to their team members, which in turn propels them toward their goal. Sadly, the terms "servant leadership" and "transformational leadership" are used so often today by charlatans as promotional tools for attracting attention and personal gain that the concepts are at risk of becoming passé and being considered a farce.

> The tragedy of our time is that we've got it backwards, we've learned to love techniques and use people.
>
> HERB KELLEHER
> Cofounder and chairman emeritus
> Southwest Airlines

When leaders of integrity understand that they have a moral obligation to be of service to others by loving, supporting, and developing those in their charge and helping move them closer to their fullest potential, they bring out the absolute best in their team—which proves to be career enhancing, life changing, and legacy building for every engaged team member. Enlightened leaders who understand this concept grasp that if they want their organizations to do great things, they must have great people on their teams. When leaders are committed to building great people first, great things happen inside *and* outside the walls and confines of their organization.

I've seen growth, promotions, raises, and wealth created among organizations that apply the principles Keith presents in this powerful book. But more important, I've seen addictions broken, careers salvaged, suicides prevented, and marriages saved when leaders commit to serving their team. You've got to get intentional about developing a culture where team members are valued and allowed to work in their strengths. That's the immeasurable bonus that comes from Keith's work and the work of others in the strengths-based community.

It's true: once these principles are applied, morale and esprit de corps spikes in the workplace, but so do dignity and self-worth in the heartplace. When a team member feels pride about the organization that provides the paycheck, while also feeling his or her positive contributions made a significant impact on the mission, morale and a sense of accomplishment soar in <u>all</u> areas of their lives.

When team members recognize that their leaders have their best interests at heart, and when they know their leaders are committed to helping them grow both professionally and personally, we see significant spikes in gratitude, morale, retention, productivity, and camaraderie. It's exciting to witness the shift in organizations when leaders finally grasp this concept, and it's absolutely rewarding (and rather addicting) to see folks move closer to their fullest potential while in our charge.

It's always been intuitive to me, but it wasn't until serving on Special Forces A-Teams in the US Army that I was able to connect the dots between working in our inherent strengths and the enhanced outcomes and mind-blowing productivity that comes from super high achievers. I miss the camaraderie from my time in Special Forces, but it's the high-octane efficiency in which a 12-man A-Team can accomplish its mission when each member is pursuing excellence and is afforded the opportunity to work within his area of natural strengths that drives me to work with leaders and high achievers today.

In 1992, I stumbled on a groundbreaking book that gave me hope that I could actually bring the efficiency and productivity of the Special Forces community into the business arena. The premise of the book was simply that people are happier and exponentially more productive when they work in their areas of strength. So, rather than forcing employees to do things they don't do well, leaders should build teams where team members support each other's strengths and augment each other's weaknesses. The book was called *Soar with Your Strengths*, by Dr. Donald O. Clifton. I was so inspired by the genius and simplicity of the strengths-based concept that I jumped at the chance to attend a three-day Varsity Management Seminar at the Gallup Organization headquarters in Omaha, Nebraska, in 1994. The seminar was taught and facilitated by the genius behind strengths-based psychology, Dr. Donald O. Clifton, himself. The warm and kindhearted Clifton (who purchased the Gallup Organization in 1988) went on to coauthor *Now, Discover Your Strengths* (with Marcus Buckingham), which ultimately led to the powerful strengths assessment we now know as *StrengthsFinder 2.0*.

Life came full circle 20 years later when the Gallup Organization, and the wonderful team at *Called to Coach*, invited me to share my story of building elite teams and high-performing organizations using the principles of strengths-based leadership on their *Called to Coach* YouTube channel. My friend Keith Baldwin has also been featured on this channel. If strengths-based initiatives, *StrengthsFinder*, or any of the terms in this foreword are foreign to you, then the ideas in the book you hold in your hands are going to prove as transformational for you as they were for me.

It was the leadership experience I gained from my military service, in concert with the concepts I learned from Clifton's books, and so eloquently illustrated in this book, that most contributed to the entrepreneurial success I've experienced to date. I can assure you, applying the principles from this book will engage your employees and propel your organization to new heights.

+ + + + +

Larry Broughton is an award-winning entrepreneur and CEO, best-selling author, and nationally recognized keynote speaker. He is the founder of yoogozi.com, broughtonHOTELS, and BROUGHTONadvisory. He has been recognized with Ernst & Young's *Entrepreneur of the Year*; NaVOBA's *Vetrepreneur of the Year*; Coastline Foundation's *Visionary of the Year*; and Passkeys Foundation's *National Business Leader of Integrity* awards. Larry is the author of *FLASHPOINTS for Achievers* and is coauthor of *VICTORY: 7 Entrepreneurial Success Strategies for Veterans*, as well as *Boots to Business* and *Introduction to Business Ownership*. He makes regular appearances on radio shows and major cable and television networks to discuss personal development, entrepreneurship, strengths-based team building, and the leadership gap he sees growing across America.

Introduction

This book is written for business owners who want to be inspired leaders and develop exceptional teams. I often provide examples from the insurance industry but these principles apply to any business. They are just as true if you substitute the name of your industry and relevant scenarios from your industry whenever you read one of my examples.

One of the foundational resources for this book is Gallup's Clifton StrengthsFinder®. As a result, references to leading a *strengths-based* business are woven throughout these chapters. After interviewing more than two million successful individuals in a variety of industries and occupations over a 30-year multimillion-dollar study, Gallup developed their Clifton StrengthsFinder®. Dr. Donald O. Clifton, the creator of this study, wanted to find out *how* highly successful people achieve success. Twenty years later, more than 11 million people have taken this assessment to discover their strengths and to learn how to develop them to achieve success.

The Clifton StrengthsFinder® is a powerful online assessment tool for identifying your natural ways of thinking, feeling, and behaving. After you take it, it will give you your own unique assessment, identifying 34 themes (a "theme" is essentially the best single word to represent a collection of hundreds of different talents that we're born with) and arranging them in order of how powerfully they show up for you specifically. This means that your strongest themes (or *strengths*, as I'll call them in this book) will be at the top of the list and those at the bottom are areas that are not as easy for you to work in.

If you haven't already, go to www.gallupstrengthscenter.com and take the assessment. You'll also receive valuable insights and tips for developing your strengths in the context of building your dream business (and life) that are specific to you personally.

WHY THIS BOOK?

I'll talk more about my background later, but first, let me explain why this book is for *you*. If you're already a business owner, you know it's a complex role. Not only can the problems and solutions of your industry be complex and varied, but running *any* business is complex. Michael Gerber, in his book *The E-Myth*, talks about the difference between working *in* a business versus working *on* a business. Even if you know a lot about your industry, you can't succeed without knowing how to run a business.

This book isn't about your industry. It's **about one element of running a business: creating an engaged team that is focused on the same results**.

As you read the chapters in this book and do the exercises, you may think, "I already know this." My question for you is *"Are you consistently performing the fundamentals that you know you should be doing, each day?"* One client hired me to hold her accountable for doing the things she already knew she should be doing! The clients who make the fastest improvement focus on two key fundamentals: simplicity and consistency. Although there are a lot of elements involved in getting your team inspired and moving in the same direction, there are a few simple elements that will drive results in your office if you focus on them daily. There is also a distinction between what your team should be doing daily and what you, the entrepreneur, should be doing daily to ensure your team is consistently taking the needed actions.

Why now? There were days when a company that had good products, good prices, and good service could be competitive. **Those days are over.** Good products, prices, and service are *expected* and are not a differentiating factor. For example, we can go online at midnight in our pajamas and request insurance quotes from multiple companies. **What makes *your* business different from others in your industry?** Unless you do something to differentiate your business from every other similar business in your town and every company that sells your products or services online, your clients will be tempted to leave you every time they see a commercial promising a 15% discount for switching over. **That difference is you and your team.** The goal of this book is to help you (and your team) be different. Get on *fire* with a burning passion to light your team up: Take action *now*! Don't wait until next year when you'll wish you had started *today*!

Increasing client retention means creating engaged customers who are less price-sensitive—that is, customers who have an emotional attachment to your team. That attachment might be to you or one of your team members, but they care about doing business with *you*. They won't switch to another company to save $117 a year because they value their relationship with Suzy or Mike or someone else in your office. They care.

In order to create clients who care, you have to create a community of team members who care. Engaged customers are the result of an engaged team. Unfortunately, though, engaged employees are rare. Gallup's research in their "State of the American Workplace" report shows that only 30% of employees in the United States are engaged at work. Those are the employees who have an emotional connection to the results of their organization. They care. They *want* to be at work. They bring their creativity, focus, ideas, and passion to the workplace. They want to make a difference.

SEVENTY PERCENT OF EMPLOYEES ARE NOT ENGAGED

Ever heard the saying "Another day, another dollar"? How about "TGIF"? These are the words of disengaged workers who *never* access their full potential. Gallup estimates that this costs the US economy between $450 and $550 *billion* a year. What's it costing you? If you have one or two employees who are not fully engaged, how much of their salary is being wasted each year? Even worse, how well are your clients being served, and what's the impact on retention, multiline sales, and referrals for your business? Even *one* disengaged employee is too many for your business. This book will present some ideas and processes to help you engage each person on your team, and yourself, so that you can create an engaged office that fosters engaged clients.

WHY ME—WHY DID *I* WRITE THIS BOOK?

I spent 26 years in the insurance business, but my last 10 were the most enlightening for me. I was in a compliance position with a large insurance company, so I traveled across multiple states conducting hundreds of reviews in many different independent insurance agencies. I was fascinated by how different each office was. In some offices, I could feel the negative energy that disengaged employees were spreading as they plodded through the day. They were burned out and felt overworked. Their production levels were significantly lower in contrast to other offices I visited, where there was a kind of frenetic activity, laughing, and excitement as the teams worked together toward common goals. At the time, I was working through a master's degree in adult education, focused on human-resource development and leadership. As I dove deep into motivation research, I was intrigued to see that the research results were completely the opposite of what many of the offices were doing: In most offices, if they focus on production at all, the only trick they have in their bag is some sort of bonus system. However, all the research proves that money by itself is *not* a successful long-term motivation strategy. I've lost track of the number of business owners who complained to me that they don't understand why their team is leaving bonus money on the table month after month.

DOES MONEY MOTIVATE YOU OVER THE LONG RUN?

For most people, the answer is "No!" More than 12 million people watched Daniel Pink's TED Talk, "The Puzzle of Motivation." He outlined three elements that must be in play to create long-term motivation: **autonomy, mastery, and purpose. That's what this book is about.**

1. *How do you create a climate that kindles your team members' natural motivation in a way that provides them freedom throughout their day to do what they do best while still being focused on your organizational goals?*
2. *How do you help team members bring out their natural strengths so they start to sense their ability to truly master their craft?*
3. *How do you help them feel they are part of something bigger than themselves and that what they do contributes to a bigger purpose?*

This book is meant to be a starting point—a guide for starting the process of inspiring your team to bring their best to work each day and also to help you bring your best every day.

MY STORY

I received very bad career advice from a career counselor early in my working life. He said, "Keith, some people don't find their inspiration at work. They just work for a paycheck and then find a sense of purpose from their social activities or family." It wasn't until I suffered my "midlife meltdown" that I realized that was horrible advice. We spend 40 to 60+ hours a week at work or thinking about work. Shouldn't we find some sense of purpose and satisfaction from all that time? I think so!

What is your level of responsibility to help your team do that? I think it's pretty high. We all have a responsibility to help our teams succeed.

I didn't always think that way; I used to think it was up to others. I *was* one of those disengaged employees; I was miserable in the job I had before compliance. One night, I came home frustrated and grouchier than normal, to say the least. My wife said, "No job is worth this; just quit!" That caught me up short. Things turned around for me after I thought, "Quit and do what?!"

"Quit and do what?" That thought haunted me as I went to sleep that night. I realized I had been feeling trapped in my job. I had been spiraling into depression. Although I was swamped at work, I always found time to stand around talking with other unhappy coworkers about how horrible our jobs were, or about the bad decisions our bosses were making. My boss even told me that he didn't know how I did my job day after day. We were claims adjusters (negotiators) for an insurance company. That is a challenging job, but continually focusing on how difficult it was to work with angry customers and attorneys wasn't solution-oriented; it was problem-oriented.

I was brought up in a hardworking family; my primary value was to work hard. For the most part, I did work hard, but I wasn't engaged in my work. I just kept doing the same thing over and over. It was my own personal *Groundhog Day* experience, extended for years. I wasn't learning the lessons. I wasn't looking for ways to be more creative, thoughtful, and effective with customers. I hadn't read a book on effective customer service skills, listening skills, or positive negotiations skills ever. My body was at work, but my heart wasn't. **I wanted to be anywhere but at work.** I was intellectually and emotionally disengaged.

I wasn't alone. I was part of the 70% of employees who are disengaged. In addition to how much money disengaged employees cost a company in lost productivity, they don't stick around. Highly engaged employees are less likely to leave a company, which reduces attrition costs. Costs related to attrition are enormous, since you have to rehire, retrain, and suffer reduced productivity during transitions.

But perhaps the biggest loss may be the wasted potential. How can we put a value on the wasted potential of employees who show up physically but don't bring their most creative and enthused self with them each day? Imagine working with a group of inspired employees who bring 100% of their ideas, creativity, and enthusiasm—employees who desire to make their work and the world better.

The benefits of being engaged are also enormous for employees. To start with, we are happier when we're engaged! Research has shown that engaged workers are more productive, happier, healthier, and more likely to be doing well in <u>multiple areas</u> of life. My reason for writing this book, and doing the coaching work I do, is to help others create engaging cultures. This book will help you think about your office and team in a new way. Sometimes new thinking is what we need to bring fresh, significant results. Let's get to it.

Section 1:

Light Your Fire

CHAPTER 1

Finding Inspiration in Your Business

If you're reading this book, it's likely that you've already thought deeply about your business. You've already put a lot of work in, and you feel some sense of accomplishment, but my questions for you are the following:

1. ***Do you feel inspired?***

Chances are you aren't feeling inspired every morning as you drive to work. You may have a vision that really charges you up, but when it comes to the nitty-gritty work of executing your objectives, tactics, and strategies, it may be a challenge to keep your "inspiration fire" burning.

What's my point? If you're not feeling inspired, you are *totally normal*. It's OK *not* to be inspired at various points of building your business. That's when the value of having a system makes itself seen in the bottom line.

It's time for a little recalibration. Let me ask you the following:

2. ***Why are you doing this in the first place?***

This begs the following, more pointed question:

3. *How do you want this business to <u>serve your life</u>?*

It comes down to what is important to you and what your life's purpose is. This isn't just about building your business. Really, it's about building your <u>life</u>.

Keeping this question near the surface as you move through this process is really helpful. There will undoubtedly be times when you are trying to hold yourself or your team members accountable for day-to-day activities but are running into some level of complacency or discouragement. Keep asking yourself, *How do I want this business to serve my life?*

Of course you're providing a service for others, but what do you want this business to do for *your* life? You need to know that. You need to know the clear and specific answer to that question. <u>That's</u> how you keep the fires of inspiration stoked!

> **If you can't tie your activities to the life you are trying to create, it will be hard to get those things done.**

You might want to read that again! Inventing the personality of your business and the way it works is a process of personal reinvention, highlighted by inspiration. It is an opportunity to align your sense of purpose with how you spend your time—a way of putting your confidence and beliefs into action.

Chances are you started your business because you want to fulfill a greater vision for yourself. In my work with agents and other small business owners, I've come to realize that really, that's all any of us want: to spend our time doing something <u>meaningful</u>. We all want inspiration to be part of our day-to-day life. Your team members *need* you to remain inspired. You're their leader!

If you're finding yourself a little frustrated or uninspired, it might be helpful to take a look at my reinvention guide. You can get a complimentary copy of this, as well as other book resources, on my website: keithbaldwin.com. Just look for the "Resources" tab at the top. Spend time walking through what you want to do in life and what you need to do to make it happen. Then, in those "dry" moments, you can access what you've learned to help you get through to the next inspiring phase. This is a great way to check in, get back to your plan, and create a team that's on fire!

CHAPTER 2

The Sweet Spot: An Introduction to Strengths

Are there some things in life that come easy to you? Easier than other things?

Of course there are! We've seen this since school—some kids seem to be naturals at sports or music, others make friends easier, and others find math a breeze. These are all clues to our talents and they start showing up early in life.

Think back to your childhood. Were there some things you just loved doing?

Were there things you did that people were amazed at and that made them say things like "That's so easy for you" or "You're a natural"?

Did you ever find time disappearing when you were in the midst of reading about something or working on a project?

Those are all clues to talent. As we find ourselves reacting to the same environment over time, responding in the same natural way each time, these talents become so strong in us that we don't even realize they are strengths. When discussing strengths with clients after they've taken Gallup's Clifton StrengthsFinder®, they will tell me things like "That can't be a strength. It's easy. Everyone can do that." Umm . . . no, not everyone can do that. The fact that something comes easy to <u>you</u> is a sign that it is one of <u>your</u> strengths. This book is meant to help you learn how to develop and focus your natural gifts, and those of your team, toward your desired results.

The challenge though, is that we are conditioned to focus on our weaknesses. Our education system, with standardized testing and standardized teaching around academic subjects, seems to assume that we're all the same, but we're not. Think about a child bringing home a report card with a D and a B. What gets the most attention? Of course, it's the D. I'm not saying we should ignore failing grades, but what if we switched our focus to the B? Encourage further development on the B subject and look for areas of crossover that may help bring the D up. Let's change our culture by helping students feel good about their natural talents, developing these gifts, and *then* focusing them toward academic achievement. If each one of us did that, it would be a start.

Once we finish school, we enter into the workforce with a whole array of required competencies and performance reviews to tell us how well we "fit" these norms. The focus is usually on identifying and "fixing" weaknesses (unless you have a gifted supervisor). While discussing research on human performance development, Gallup's CEO Jim Clifton told students at Georgetown University that once a supervisor starts "helping" their employee fix their weaknesses, growth stops. The **only meaningful growth** comes from focusing on people's natural strengths and then focusing them toward organizational results.

Extensive research has shown that development **slows down** once you go into a performance discussion that has the goal of changing who you are. Yet we buy into the myth that this is what we "should" do!

I remember one performance review I felt really good about . . . until the end. My supervisor spent a lot of time praising my work in the prior year; then we got to the last page of my performance review, and there was a big empty box titled "Needs Improvement." My boss <u>had</u> to put something in there because the bosses up the line **expected** this space to be filled with a weakness that I was going to work on during the next year. We wrote something in there *and nothing changed*.

What if instead the box said "Next Year's Focus"? Then we could have had a meaningful conversation about my natural strengths—that is, how I could improve on them and how I could focus them toward meeting organizational goals? *That* would be an entirely new type of conversation.

The key to success, the real sweet spot, is to identify and understand your own strengths, develop them, and direct these natural abilities toward the results that are important to you and your organization.

Remember, the first step is to take Gallup's Clifton StrengthsFinder®. You'll reach a new level of understanding your own strengths after taking the assessment and reading the reports that come with it.

But that is just the starting point. Think of athletes who are incredibly gifted. Don't they **continually** invest in their natural gifts? Of course they do. Professional athletes have coaches to give them performance feedback, they add new skills, they study their craft to increase their knowledge, and they practice—over and over and over again. We should do no less.

If your role is to inspire a team of sales professionals in your office, what skills do you need to develop to become more effective?

How do you practice motivating and developing others? How often should you do it?

What new knowledge do you need?

After you identify your strengths, your approach will be different from other entrepreneurs you know. Because, well, you *are* different. Read your strengths report and consider how you will use your top five strengths to help your team be more effective at what they do.

Some people reading this may have the impression that strengths development and deployment is "soft." It is not. **This is not about letting go of results.** Developing a strengths-based leadership approach in your company involves *separating what needs to be done from how it will be done.* We'll talk more about that in later chapters, but it is crucial that you identify the results you expect from each employee. Then it is your role to work with each employee to help them learn how to aim their talents toward those results. For most people, their personal strengths are yet not fully utilized because they just feel so natural. Why focus on that? Because that's where your biggest return on investment lies!

Gallup makes a distinction between talents and strengths. The Clifton StrengthsFinder® identifies strengths potential: our natural ways of thinking, feeling, and behaving. On a scale of 1–10, a 10/true strength is when we obtain near perfect results consistently in some given activity. This only happens when we consistently aim our strengths toward our role—in your case, as a business owner or leader.

Section 2:

Lead from Strengths

CHAPTER 3

The Spark of a Well-Rounded Team

Strengths-based leadership is first about knowing your own strengths and cultivating them in a way that helps support your personal and professional goals. But that's just the beginning. The second component of leading from your strengths involves knowing your team's strengths.

It's *all* about understanding the strengths and talents of your team. We are all "wired" differently, and that's part of what we pride ourselves on. Other people see the world and react to it in a variety of ways—most often differently than how we ourselves would. Everyone seems to acknowledge that easily, but until you start deeply appreciating strengths and gaining an understanding of how you can *focus* your team's natural talents toward the results you want, you can't fully understand the beauty and benefits of that diversity.

INDIVIDUALS ARE NOT WELL-ROUNDED, BUT TEAMS MUST BE

Some people are better at some things than others. Although we'd all like to be good at everything, most of us realize that having that expectation of ourselves is crazy. That's the beauty of a well-rounded team. If you build your team based on the strengths of the individuals, then your strengths combine and complement each other in a way that moves you all forward.

When you are looking at your team, it's important to consider how *each* person's strengths can contribute to your collective success. The best place to start is by having everyone take Gallup's Clifton Strengths-Finder® assessment.

I've mentioned the 34 themes that Gallup identified based on extensive research. **These themes (collections of talents) are not strengths until we develop them.** The chances of someone having the same top five themes/strengths as you, in the same order, are about 1 in 33 million!

What's the point? We each fill a unique niche on a team based not just on our role, but on our talents too. Knowing what that combination is helps us develop *a communal, razor-sharp focus on **how** the team is going to meet our objectives.*

It can be overwhelming to look at everyone's individual strengths report and then figure out how those strengths combinations are going to work together for success. In terms of the big picture, Gallup found that the 34 strengths contribute to organizational goals in four different domains.

Executing	Influencing	Relationship Building	Strategic Thinking
Achiever	Activator	Adaptability	Analytical
Arranger	Command	Connectedness	Context
Belief	Communication	Developer	Futuristic
Consistency	Competition	Empathy	Ideation
Deliberative	Maximizer	Harmony	Input
Discipline	Self-Assurance	Includer	Intellection
Focus	Significance	Individualization	Learner
Responsibility	Woo	Positivity	Strategic
Restorative		Relator	

See the Bibliography for resources to understand all 34 Talent Themes/Strengths in the bottom row.

It's helpful to look at your team in the context of these *Four Domains of Strengths*:

1. **Executing:** People with themes in this area have the talent to make things happen. They turn thoughts into action.
2. **Influencing:** Those with influencing themes have the ability to sway others and move the team forward. They are often the ones to take charge, speak up, and shape results.
3. **Relationship Building:** Team members with these strengths can be the social glue that holds a team together and develops deep relationships with customers.
4. **Strategic Thinking:** These are the people who can see the way forward; they'll consider multiple options and help the team plan the way to success.

You can see that all four of these domains are important in any business. But often I find that no one person is strong in all the areas. That's OK! The question for *you* is "How will we account for all four areas getting covered on our *team*?" When you are gathering your team, it's important to think about the necessity of covering each of those four areas.

WELL-ROUNDED TEAMS WEAR THE RIGHT HATS

When you start looking at strengths from the team perspective and identifying who is best at what, then you can ensure that the right people are in the right roles, based on what they're naturally good at and *love* to do. Essentially, *it's about allowing people to flourish* rather than trying to fit a square peg in a round hole.

In his book *Good to Great*, Jim Collins coined the phrase **"Getting the right people on the bus and the right people in the right seats"** to describe this process.

Highly successful organizations, first and foremost, hire for talent. They select the right employees, then they make sure those employees are "in the right seats on the bus"—that is, they're in the right roles for their strengths.

Once you've analyzed the strengths of your team members, you've discovered where they shine. Most likely, you hadn't seen that before. Your next step is to help them apply their strengths to daily tactics that will help achieve the group objective. Sometimes you have to let them try on different hats to see which role allows their strengths to shine the most, but the point is *leading from your strengths* means wearing a hat (or two) that fits you and letting others don the hat that fits them best. This is where you empower your team members not only to be fully engaged in their work life but also to design, implement, and solve problems in *all* areas of their lives. They'll appreciate that and your efforts to understand them.

Strengthening talents we're born with is inspiring and exciting. Trying to "correct" our weaknesses is hard and frustrating. That's because the latter work focuses on what we do *not* naturally possess—gifts we were not given. When you look for the gifts your employees *were* given and recognize them verbally, people feel "seen" and appreciated for who they are. **A person who feels appreciated will do all they can for you** and is more likely to be <u>fully</u> engaged in the mission.

CHAPTER 4

The Business Success Wheel©:
A Tool to Drive Success

When we take the time to get specific about our goals and examine our resources, it's inevitable that we will find ourselves inspired to take action. That's a great motivator, but the reality is that affecting change takes a **deliberate strategy** and **consistent effort** over time. That's why I developed the Business Success Wheel©.

My Business Success Wheel© is modeled after the Wheel of Life, but it focuses on key areas that drive results in a business. These are areas that when focused on, enable business leaders to know exactly where they are and in which areas they need to improve.

For instance, when we use the Wheel of Life, we ask, *What does success in life mean to me?* The Wheel of Life typically has categories such as the following:

- work/career
- mental/personal development
- spirituality
- health
- relationships/social
- physical environment
- relaxation/play

Obviously, more than one thing drives our success and happiness in life. Similarly, the Business Success Wheel© looks at a range of factors. The idea is that you achieve fulfillment of the mission when you've reached a good level of satisfaction in **each** of the areas (in a balanced manner). Then you keep getting better by making improvements in each area, all the time.

Take a look at the Business Success Wheel© on page 18. The areas I've included have proven to be important for business leadership success. Every business leader has a slightly different office or environment, so you may want to add to or subtract categories according to your preferences. Some of the items on the wheel drive results more than others, but it's important to remember that *all* these areas are connected. When we only focus on one or two areas, it causes a deficit in the other areas and we suffer the consequences. It's more effective to be aware of all the critical areas and **remain accountable for achieving balance while you achieve success**; then your success will be long-term rather than short-lived.

HOW TO USE THE BUSINESS SUCCESS WHEEL©

Make sure it reflects areas that are important to your team by taking the following steps:

1. Ask two questions about each area: How successful or how satisfied am I in that area? How successful are we at implementing these areas in our office environment?
2. Rate each one of these areas for yourself from a 1 to 10. Ten means you're knocking it out of the park and you can't imagine anything being better. One means you are not satisfied in that area at all.
   This is a very subjective and personal measurement, but *you* are the leader of your business. With similar objective results, one business owner may be entirely satisfied and another business owner may be really dissatisfied. The key is just to get your rating on paper and start there.
3. Ask yourself what a slight improvement would look like. For example, if you rate your income generating activities at a 5, what would a 6 look like? Describe it.

4. Determine in detail what you need to do to achieve that slight increase.
5. Develop an action plan to make it happen. Include names and deadlines. Delegate authority, responsibility, and resources.

The Business Success Wheel© is a tool to help you continually work toward *your* vision of success. In essence, this is *kaizen*. **Kaizen is good!**

Kaizen: This is a word that became a popular management term when the Japanese auto industry went from being average to being the best in the world. It refers to continual change or continuous improvement.

Growth becomes very manageable when we start by making small improvements toward clearly defined mileposts or objectives. If we think about life in general, we realize that big results don't normally come from one defining moment in life. The vast majority of our success comes from small incremental improvements that we make, day in and day out.

Take a snapshot of your business now with this Business Success Wheel©. Date it. Do this over and over—once a month or at least once a quarter—and see your growth!

Remember:

"We succeed when we make continuous small improvements."

and

"What gets measured improves."

Business Success Wheel©

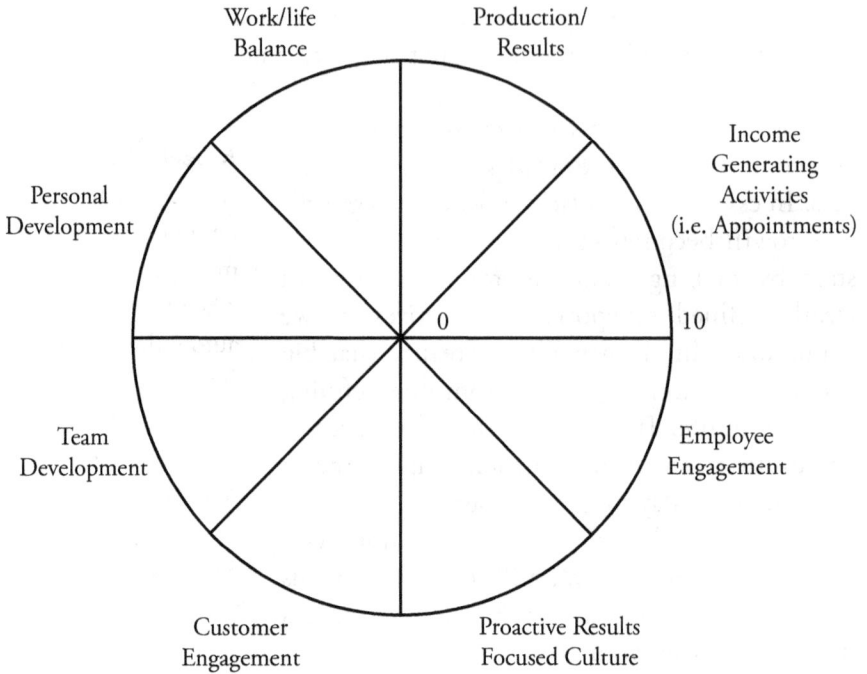

Work/life Balance

Production/ Results

Income Generating Activities (i.e. Appointments)

Personal Development

0   10

Team Development

Employee Engagement

Customer Engagement

Proactive Results Focused Culture

<table>
<tr><td>WHEEL INSTRUCTIONS</td><td>EXAMPLE</td></tr>
</table>

The 8 sections in the Wheel represent your ideal vision.

Change, add, or rename any category as needed.

Next, taking the center of the wheel as 0 and the outer edge as 10, rank your **level of satisfaction** with each area out of 10 by drawing a straight or curved line to create a new outer edge (see example).

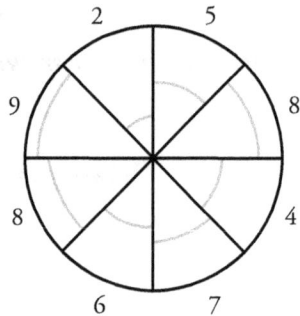

2   5

9   8

8   4

6   7

Chapter 5

Strengths-Based Business Leadership

HOW DO YOU OR COULD YOU LEAD YOUR BUSINESS WITH A PURPOSEFUL FOCUS ON YOUR UNIQUE STRENGTHS?

A key premise of this book is that we all have unique strengths to use toward creating success in life. Highly successful individuals are nearly always not well-rounded, but teams **must** be. Part of your role in creating an exceptional business is to develop your own strengths and focus them toward creating a well-rounded, strengths-based team.

The starting point is with you. How do you lead best? The research that formed the foundation of Gallup's book *Strengths Based Leadership* found that **the very best leaders** lead in different ways. They've learned their unique talents, developed skills and knowledge around leadership, and then focused their strengths to create vibrant, successful organizations. I've found the same experience working with different business leaders. The very best learn how to lead their team in a way that is natural to them and partner with others to fill in the gaps.

One of the keys for developing strengths is to **become very purposeful about what results you are trying to create**. Then think about how to use your strengths to get those results. We all have areas of strengths and areas that aren't so strong. Let's take another look at the domains and strength themes that Gallup identified in the context of what it takes to develop and maintain a highly successful business.

Here are several key tactics to consider:

1. Develop a strategy to develop and/or maximize your company's scorecard or other bonus systems. Implement that strategy consistently.
2. Create systems in your business to ensure exceptional customer service.
3. Identify the strengths needed and locate the right team members for your office.
4. Train each team member to be exceptional, based on their own unique strengths.
5. Discuss how these strengths work together in your own team in order to develop a cohesive team that works well together.
6. Hold people accountable to maintain consistency in activities that drive results.
7. Develop relationships in your community that keep the phone ringing.

Which of these seem easy to you? Which do you find yourself putting off or not doing consistently? Self-honesty is important here. One of my mentors, Larry Broughton, is fond of saying, **"Reality is our friend."**

Often though, we'd rather not think about it, especially if it means we aren't good at something. Think about these key tactics and read through the four domains again, as well as your own strengths report. *Where do you excel in the Four Domains of Strengths?*

Refer back to your Gallup Clifton StrengthsFinder® assessment results and look at the descriptions in Chapter 3. Think about what seems easy to you. When you consider the areas you are strongest in, how would you apply those strengths toward the key elements of creating a highly engaged team? In Section 6 of this book, I'll offer some best practices, but for now, start thinking about some of your natural strengths and how they could be utilized to build a strong team. As mentioned before, it's crucial to separate **what** needs to be done from **how** you do it.

Business leaders have two roles. You, of course, want to reach your business objectives by getting the work done through your team. However, you can only do that by developing the people in the context of the work that needs to be done. As philanthropist Agha Hasan Abedi once said, "The conventional definition of management is getting work done through people, but **real management is developing people** through work."

When you start to think that your primary role as a leader is to develop the people on your team, what activities come to mind? I'll give you some ideas in Sections 4 and 5, but for now, just think about what needs to be done to train, inspire, and focus your team on those activities that directly lead to reaching business goals. If you made a list of all the activities you'd need to do consistently to develop your team, you'd likely come up with things like the following:

- clarifying expectations
- catching employees doing things right
- weekly accountability reports and spot coaching
- monthly developmental conversations with each team member
- learning and bonding opportunities to create an informed and inspired culture

HOW CAN YOU ENSURE THESE ACTIVITIES OCCUR, BASED ON YOUR UNIQUE STRENGTHS?

When you start to think about the type of business you want to have and what activities need to occur to create that business, you will likely come up with a long list. Begin by focusing on **your** strengths. I'll give you exercises in the next two chapters, but for now, make a list of all the essential actions of an exceptional business leader. Then look at that list and break it into the following three areas:

1. Must do (or else we won't succeed)
2. Would be nice to do (in order to reach maximum levels of success)
3. Could do (but won't have a significant impact on our results)

Focus first on the "Must Do" area. *Which of these fall within your strengths?* Create a strategy for three of the items on the "Must Do" list, using one or more of your strengths.

Let's move on to the keys for leveraging your strengths.

CHAPTER 6

Three Steps to Igniting Your Strengths

Now that I've introduced the concept of leading your business from your strengths, and you've taken the Gallup Clifton StrengthsFinder® assessment, what do you do?

1. Go over your results report, the guides provided to help you develop your personal strengths, and other resources in the Gallup online portal www.gallupstrengthscenter.com. Watch their "Strengths Exploration" videos about your top five strengths (or more, if you are ambitious). Gallup also provides "Theme Thursdays" on their YouTube channel to help you understand strengths.
2. Look at your plan for growth through the lens of your own unique strengths. It's really interesting to go back to your plan and reconsider how you can use your strengths to better plan and implement your systems. It's useful to ask, "Based on my strengths, how can I get the results I've identified?"
3. Start with yourself. It's easy to get excited about identifying and leveraging the variety of strengths offered by your entire team, but you must start with yourself. Once you get clarity about where your natural talents are (and your **blind spots**, which will be areas on the bottom of your assessment results), then you can begin to effectively integrate

your team's talents. In order to communicate well with your team and authentically involve them in your planning process, you must have this kind of understanding about yourself first. This is a deeply introspective exercise. It's an unmasking, so to speak, and it can be very freeing because it gives you a clearer picture of why your efforts may or may not have succeeded in the past. There has to be an order of magnitude to create your list, and the order in which the strength themes are listed on the assessment result will be different for each person. If you accept that fact, you can successfully develop a dynamic team where each person is truly appreciated for what they bring to the table.

A word about "Blind Spots." When I talk about blind spots, I am talking about those themes or strengths that show up low on your list of 34. The key is not to focus on those as weaknesses—emphasize your strengths first—but it is beneficial to be aware of them. How so? First ask yourself if you are achieving your results based on using your strengths or if it feels like a battle. If you are applying your natural strengths but still not getting the results you want, then it's time to look at your blind spots to figure out how you can manage around them. You can't improve on your blind spots by trying to change something that doesn't come naturally to you. Instead, look at the result you want and see how the strengths at the top of your list can help you achieve it, perhaps in a different way than you think "most people" would. Only after you understand your own strengths and have actually applied them toward your desired results can you effectively work to build an engaged team that leverages every member's individual strengths to the utmost.

It's been my experience that detail work and follow-up doesn't come naturally to many business leaders, and they beat themselves up about it: *"I should be able to do this." "I should be able to keep track of all this stuff."*

But if it's simply not one of your natural talents, that's OK. It just means that someone else on your team will need to have a natural talent for details or follow-up, so you can focus on leveraging your own talents.

As another example of managing around our "weaknesses," let's say you don't have a passion for cold calling. No problem—find someone with a natural talent that Gallup calls "WOO," which is someone who really feels good about getting to know new people and *Winning Others Over.*

CHAPTER 7

How Your Talents Become Strengths

By now, you've probably figured out the things that come easily to you and the things that are a struggle. Essentially, we all arrive with our own unique raw talents.

A talent is basically "the way we naturally think, feel and behave" or "a natural inclination." These play out in how we react to our environment. A talent becomes a strength as we practice focusing it toward the results we are trying to achieve.

This practice provides the foundation for leading from our strengths. When we develop a keen, introspective understanding of our natural talents and develop them through practice, increased knowledge, and skill development, we have taken the first steps in leveraging those talents for success.

HOW?

We all have a vague sense of what our talents might be, but it's more effective if we can be specific so we truly understand, appreciate, and improve on them.

Let's go a little deeper on what we talked about in Chapter 2. Think back over your life and look for clues to your talents such as the following:

- Were there things that were really easy to learn?
- Are there activities that you gain great satisfaction from doing?
- Is there something that you finish and can't wait to do again?
- Are there things that are naturally easy for you? Things that people often complement you on by saying, "You're so good at that!" or "That seems to come really easy to you!"?
- Are there activities you perform where time just disappears because you are so engrossed in them?

Start paying attention to those things! Look at them through the lens of the results from your strengths assessment.

The next step is to think about how you could purposefully use those talents to gain the results you want. *One way* to turn a talent into a strength is by learning more about a specific topic or subject that relates to your work.

For example, as I mentioned, I used to negotiate insurance claims, so I frequently worked with upset people. At first, I would try to confront people head-on with the facts, because those are the terms I naturally think in. It didn't work very well. I had a lot of arguments and genuinely hated my job.

After the "discussion" with my wife, I regained my sense of freedom, and I realized I needed to start taking responsibility for my own thoughts. I started to look for ways to become more effective and learn how to build rapport with angry people. Part of that effort required me to identify my talents and part of it involved studying communication, negotiation, and conflict resolution. I took my natural talents and put effort into becoming skilled at applying them. I studied interpersonal communication, effective listening, and how to influence people. I became deliberate about how I used my *natural* ability to calm people and began using it in my role. Harmony is one of my top strengths, so I often asked myself, "How can I find the common ground in this situation?" Usually it was by taking a moment to put myself in their shoes. I validated their feelings, even if I didn't agree with their point of view. I had a sincere desire to make the best of the situation for both of us. These efforts made a difference for me and my clients— I used a combination of talent, practice, and increased knowledge. People could feel my sincere desire to help and therefore made more reasonable requests.

Another way to think about talents is to revisit the context of professional athletes: There are many gifted athletes in a variety of sports with a variety of different talents. Some end up in the Olympics or on television. They wouldn't get there if they didn't practice diligently. On the other hand, there are some athletes who work diligently 12 hours a day, read the books, study the techniques, and hire coaches; they *really* try, but if they don't have that natural talent, they will never be "world class" in that particular sport.

The world tells us that we can be anything we want, and we want to believe that, but it's not entirely true and that's OK! The truth is, we are all much happier when we are fulfilling roles that engage our natural talents. Luckily, those are usually roles that we **want** to fill. We can achieve incredible results, far beyond what we ever dreamed for ourselves, but we can't be *any*thing. Our true power comes when we develop our natural talents and then focus them toward desired results. Combining talent, skill, and knowledge with focus on our desired result produces incredible achievements!

Section 3:

Build a 90-Day Game Plan

CHAPTER 8

Three Steps to a Business Plan That Sees the Light of Day

KEEP IT SIMPLE!

Something I really enjoy about my life as a coach is recognizing the common challenges we all face in business, regardless of profession, and finding ways to address those challenges.

When I begin working with a client, I want to get a sense of where we are starting from so we don't try to address challenges that have already been addressed and spin our wheels. I often start this conversation with "Let's take a look at your business plan."

There seems to be an epidemic of *business plan shame*! The response typically begins with a sheepish look, along with a little mumbling, and then the truth comes out: they don't have a plan, or if they do, they haven't looked at it for eight months and aren't sure where to find it. Some people, at that point, throw themselves on the floor and begin to sob. Okay, so it's not that dramatic, but you get the point. The plan, if it exists, is probably lurking in a cabinet or Dropbox folder somewhere and has become this big, daunting thing gathering the dust of neglect. It's pretty clear the plan isn't *working*.

That's one of the problems with *big* business plans for *small* businesses: they don't get put to work. A plan is only as good as its implementation.

For small business owners, a business plan designed for a major company is simply too cumbersome to implement. That's nothing to be ashamed about!

It comes down to resources: big companies can break a multipage plan into manageable parts, delegate those parts to the appropriate team members, and then see the plan through, because no one person is stuck with too much on their plate. But as a business leader, you are responsible for **everything** about the way your business works.

What's the solution? Keep it simple.

Here are three steps to a business plan that **works** for your business:

1. **Develop a one-page plan.** That already sounds more manageable, doesn't it? We'll talk about the foundation of your plan here, but I also recommend the book *The One Hour Plan for Growth* by Joe Calhoon. It describes, in detail, the value of a one-page plan and the best method for developing one. One of the biggest benefits is that a one-page plan helps you stay focused on the key activities that will lead to accomplishing your larger goals.
2. **Incorporate it into your meetings.** The beauty of a one-page plan is that you can make it an integral part of your team meetings and your employee coaching sessions. It only requires minutes of your attention at a time, not hours. For example, at your weekly team meetings, you can have a roundtable discussion in which each member states one task they accomplished and one thing they are working on *in direct relation to the plan*. It's about focusing your activities.
3. **Think of it as a working document, not a static document.** Your one-page plan can easily become a living piece of your business. As your team focuses on it, you will all move the ball forward. Goals and priorities will shift to accommodate your growth. Progress is more easily realized, and progress feels really good—that feeling motivates everyone to keep getting better!

If you have a business plan hidden in a closet, maybe it's OK to just let sleeping dragons lie. Unless you need financing, you don't need a thorough plan; you just need a plan that will help you focus on key initiatives that lead you to your goals over the next 90 days and beyond. There are a lot of resources online to do this, but I've included a sample on the next page. We'll walk through the key elements to focus on next.

Your 90-Day Game Plan

	Strategies	Tactics
Vision		
Mission		
Values		
Objectives		

CHAPTER 9

Vision/Mission/Values

VISION: THE FOUNDATION OF YOUR BUSINESS PLAN

You're probably familiar with the idea of a *vision* in regards to your business. If you've participated in any kind of strategic planning, you've heard a lot about vision, mission, goals, and objectives. Vision is foundational to long-term success because running a business requires a lot of a person. Identifying what you really want is crucial to your ultimate success. If you spend your time and energy on tasks that don't match your vision, it can lessen your feeling of fulfillment and thus cause a great deal of stress for you.

What Is the Purpose of a Vision?

Vision is about creating a compelling picture of your future. In the end, it should be inspiring to you. It can be one of the following:

- something that you really want to make a reality
- who you want to become (not necessarily who you are now)
- something that pulls you like a magnet

It can be all these things tied together. In fact, the more of these elements it involves, the clearer it becomes. When you have a clear, specific vision written out, it gives you something to measure against everything you do. Even if you are feeling burned out or overwhelmed (which can happen), your vision can reinvigorate and excite you. You can step back and look at that vision to remind yourself of why you are doing all that you're doing. **Vision is the very foundation of your business plan** (and often of your life plan).

How Do You Start Creating Your Vision?

The best thing to do is to start asking yourself questions like the following:

What excites me about opening a business?

What does my ideal business look like?

What do I want my position as leader to look like?
     Get specific. This is meant to be a fun exercise. Don't limit yourself by "ifs" or limit yourself based on your current realities. This is the dreaming part.

What does it feel like when customers walk through the door of my business?
     Maybe people feel at ease: the space is open, clean, and tidy. Everyone is greeted as soon as they walk in, and they feel more like they are walking into the home of a friend than a business. Maybe the feel is less casual, but no less professional or friendly.

*What does it feel like when **I** walk in the door?*
     This is equally important.

What kind of work environment or relationships do I want to create?
     Do you want to hear people laughing? Perhaps you want an atmosphere of camaraderie and you want to feel like your coworkers and employees are comfortable approaching you with any question. Maybe having a lot of windows and a comfortable common area is really important to you. Details are what make your vision yours.

What are customer interactions like?

What am I providing? Trusted advisors in a positive environment? Peace of mind?

What markets do I serve?

How do I want others to describe my business?

What is my area of expertise?

Do I want to be more of a generalist or would I prefer to offer niche services?

Who are my customers?

What types of customers do I want to work with most of the time? Doing what?

When you answer these questions, you will be able to shape those answers into a statement about one or two sentences long. This should be the answer that you provide to people who ask you what you do. The answer is your vision, not your job title. Your vision attracts new clients to you. The beautiful thing about your vision is that it evolves with you and your business. The most important thing is that you feel really good about it. So go ahead, start putting your vision to paper. The sooner you do, the sooner it will become your reality.

THE WHY AND HOW OF A MISSION STATEMENT

What Is a Mission Statement?

We've talked about the importance of having a vision and how it's a central element to a business plan. Having a mission is equally important, and it's tied closely to your vision because they are both about giving you something to strive for. Yet the primary difference between the two is this: **Vision is about where we're going and mission is what we're doing right now.**

A mission statement defines why you exist **now**. When you think about it, it makes sense that it would be a central element to your plan—it's a central element in life. We all seek purpose. A mission helps us define, remember, and articulate that purpose.

How Do You Develop a Mission Statement?

When you think about creating a mission statement, consider the following:

- what you do for customers
- what your purpose is for being here (for existing)
- how you are different from the competition
- how you **want to be** different from your competitors
- why is any of that important

Another way to look at it is to ask yourself, *"If I knew I could not fail, what would I be doing? Why is that important to my clients?"*

There can be no doubt in a mission. Focus on developing a unifying statement that defines what you do *now* and why you do it. This brings clarity and confidence.

It's also helpful to think of it from the perspective of your customers or clients: *What is your "brand promise"? How are you different than other people who provide the same service or commodity?*

For example, if you are an insurance agent, how do you want your customers to describe you? Do you want them to make statements like the following?

- "I can contact my agent whenever I have a question, and she always goes above and beyond to respond in a timely fashion and gives me an answer I can understand."
- "I feel safer knowing that my agent has helped me find a policy that will cover me if anything bad ever happens to my personal property or my family."
- "I don't understand insurance at all, but my agent explains it to me in terms I can understand, and he has helped me make informed decisions."
- "You should call my agent, she is so helpful and I totally trust her!"

When you look at these statements, it's easier to see why you exist. Perhaps your first-draft mission statement would be something like this:

To serve as a resource and a refuge for our clients and to provide the best protection in times of great need.

As with vision, it's important to **keep your mission statement brief and pointed**, so everyone on your team can easily call it to mind and focus on it.

How Do You Implement a Mission Statement?

The beautiful thing about a mission statement is that it is (or should be) easy to remember and recite. It is a great tool for measuring our daily successes. Two ways you can keep your mission *alive* are the following:

- Integrate it into your meeting agendas. Take a few moments at each meeting and ask each team member to name three actions they've taken throughout the week to support your mission.
- Post it for yourselves and your clients. When your mission is constantly in view, you can't help but keep your eye on the ball. When your clients see it, they know what they can expect and feel comforted that your mission is on the forefront of your mind.

Once you develop a strong vision and mission, you are poised to direct your actions to fulfill both and, ultimately, to experience the level of success you dream of.

CORE VALUES: HOW WE WORK

An important part of defining how you want your business to operate is about defining the values that are important to you as a leader, as well as to your team. These are the guiding principles you won't compromise—not even for your best customers or in the worst of times. These are your **core values**. You may be able to understand and implement them better if you think of them as unifying truths that the whole office can focus on daily.

It's likely that there are numerous values that feed into your mission and vision, but narrowing your list down to a few **core** values helps you more successfully focus when implementing your plan. This will allow you to serve your customers in the best way possible.

The three together—vision, mission, and core values—truly narrow your focus on the target. They provide a clear framework for everyone to work within so that you can execute your plan most efficiently and successfully.

How Do You Identify Your Core Values?

In my work with all sorts of business owners, I've seen great success in identifying core values by working through the following values exercise:

1. Start with the list of values on page 42.
2. Go through that list and circle those you believe in.
3. Add any that you think are important that aren't included on the list.
4. Narrow it down; choose 10 that you can't live without.
5. Then narrow it down again—to five.

I know this sounds daunting because we all have numerous values. It is hard not to feel like we're giving something up when we have to prioritize them. But I promise, having fewer values to focus on will help you embody them. By doing that you will probably automatically employ the rest of your values as well.

It's Better to Do a Few Things Really Well than to Be Mediocre at Many Things

Your values may shift slightly over time, but those that you identify as your core values are long lasting. They are those values that are near and dear to your heart. You can be true to yourself best by consciously choosing them as a code to live by. Choosing your top five values makes all other decisions a lot easier!

Get started and determine your core values. This is a great exercise to do with your team. Photocopy it or print it out from my website and give it to each one of your team members. Then go over the results with your team and decide together which of everyone's top five will represent the top five for the team.

What Do I Do Once We Have Our Core Values?

1. Laminate them for each team member and keep them visible—on your desks, in your common space, or wherever you will see them daily.
2. Discuss how to live them. For example, say *kindness* and *service* are both on your list of core values. You need to ask yourselves how you would employ them in different scenarios. What if a customer is having a really bad day and they take it out on you or one of your coworkers? How would you live your core values in that situation? How do you live your core values day in and day out, with your clients and with each other?
3. Make them a routine part of your team meeting. Ask your team members how what they've done throughout the week illustrates that they've lived those core values.

Your vision, mission, and core values compose the foundation of your business plan. It's important to keep them top of mind for you and your team. You are creating a living, breathing document that dictates how you operate. When you take the time to develop each component with a lot of input from your team, you are investing in your success and creating something that you all can buy into.

Core Values Exercise

1. Review the list of values and circle those that are most important to you.
2. Add other values that are important to you.
3. Review those that are circled and put a checkmark by *10* that you can't do without.
4. Finally, narrow the list down to your top five values. Do this by comparing each of the top 10 values while asking, "If I could have this one, but not the other would I be OK with that?" For instance, if I could have *challenge*, but not *freedom*, is that OK for me?
5. List your top five values.

❑ Accomplishment	❑ Focus	❑ Peace
❑ Accuracy	❑ Forgiveness	❑ Presence
❑ Acknowledgement	❑ Freedom	❑ Productivity
❑ Adventure	❑ Friendship	❑ Recognition
❑ Authenticity	❑ Fun	❑ Respect
❑ Balance	❑ Generosity	❑ Resourcefulness
❑ Beauty	❑ Gentleness	❑ Romance
❑ Boldness	❑ Growth	❑ Safety
❑ Calm	❑ Happiness	❑ Self-Esteem
❑ Challenge	❑ Harmony	❑ Service
❑ Collaboration	❑ Health	❑ Simplicity
❑ Community	❑ Helpfulness	❑ Spirituality
❑ Compassion	❑ Honesty	❑ Spontaneity
❑ Comradeship	❑ Honor	❑ Strength
❑ Confidence	❑ Humor	❑ Tact
❑ Connectedness	❑ Idealism	❑ Thankfulness
❑ Contentment	❑ Independence	❑ Tolerance
❑ Contribution	❑ Innovation	❑ Tradition
❑ Cooperation	❑ Integrity	❑ Trust
❑ Courage	❑ Intuition	❑ Understanding
❑ Creativity	❑ Joy	❑ Unity
❑ Curiosity	❑ Kindness	❑ Vitality
❑ Determination	❑ Learning	❑ Wisdom
❑ Directness	❑ Listening	❑ _____
❑ Discovery	❑ Love	❑ _____
❑ Ease	❑ Loyalty	
❑ Effortlessness	❑ Optimism	***Top Five Values:***
❑ Empowerment	❑ Orderliness	1. _____
❑ Enthusiasm	❑ Participation	2. _____
❑ Environment	❑ Partnership	3. _____
❑ Excellence	❑ Passion	4. _____
❑ Fairness	❑ Patience	5. _____
❑ Flexibility		

CHAPTER 10

Objectives/Strategies/Tactics

THREE KEYS TO DEVELOPING OBJECTIVES AS A TRUE MEASURE OF SUCCESS

Once you've identified the foundational components of your business plan, the inevitable question arises: *Now what?* More specifically, *How do I know when I am actually achieving my vision and mission **and** working by my core values?*

Enter *objectives*. Objectives are what help us measure our success, and they are the best measure of success when they are developed using the following three key tactics:

1. **Be SMART.** You're probably already be familiar with this approach, but just in case, let's review:

SMART is an acronym for

Specific
In as much detail as possible, describe what you will do. Think of *what*, *where*, *how* and *who* else may need to be involved.

Measurable
Exactly how will you know you've accomplished the objective? How will you measure success? Is this subjective or can someone else see the measurement the same way?

Action-Oriented
Is your written goal something to act on?

Realistic
Is it possible to take action on this now? Do I have everything I need?

Time-Oriented
When will you finish? Are there milestones along the way that you
can pinpoint?

When you start to develop your objectives, it's helpful to check them
and make sure they are SMART. For example, if you want to increase the
number of life insurance policies you sell as a team, you should choose
a certain number that you believe you can accomplish and put it in a
specific timeframe.* Say you are establishing your goals at the beginning
of 2016, and you sold 60 life insurance policies in 2015. You've added
additional team members with proven sales talent. Then your objective
might look like this:

Sell 99 life insurance policies by November 2016. On average, the
target is nine life insurance policies a month. Split that by three financial services team members, and that's three life insurance policies per
month per team member.

2. **Maximize the Benefit.** As a business owner, you often get pulled in
   many directions, and your to-do list is a mile long. Yet you see the
   greatest results when you are able to focus on just a *few* things. So
   when you develop your objectives, it can also be really helpful to
   do a simple exercise:

Ask yourself, *If everything else stayed the same,* **what 1–3 things would
have the biggest benefit** to *my business if I focused consistently and intently
on those 1–3 things?*

Another way to look at it is this: *What would give us the biggest bang
for our buck?*

---

* It is important to assign a timeframe based on what time of year (or what part of your
fiscal year) you are in and make sure that you give yourselves enough time to accomplish
the objective. The timeframe can inform how realistic and achievable your objectives are.

In this case, replace bucks with time. Some people would argue they are the same thing!

That reminds me of a great example for how to view your objectives: A very successful salesperson told me once that it occurred to him that every "no" was worth money. He looked at several months of sales results and divided that by the number of phone calls he made during that time. He figured out that every call he made was worth $10 to his business—regardless of whether the person he called said "yes" or "no" or simply hung up on him. Every call and appointment he made got him closer to a big sale, so **every** call was worth money, even the nos. **Consistent action** (on the **right** thing) is what's important, not the result of each specific action. This is a key thing to keep in mind.

ESTABLISH ALIGNMENT

Once you've developed your objectives based on your 1–3 areas of focus and built them within the framework of the SMART approach, it's important to go back and compare them with your vision, mission, and core values.

Will focusing on this particular thing get me closer to my vision (like the phone calls did for the agent I just mentioned)? When you take the time to do this, you are clarifying for yourself and for your team what "the right things" are. You're planting the seeds that will help your business grow into your vision. You are also beginning to build an engaged team. When your team sees your 100% commitment to the vision, mission, and core values—the meaning behind the work—they are more likely to be inspired and motivated. By also having clarity about which specific activities are *most* important, they will be better able to see their role in the success of the team. This is how you link what you do every day to

- who you are,
- what you want to be, and
- what you want your business to be about.

It demonstrates the direct value of the tasks you do daily (which aren't always something you are excited about!). Alignment creates momentum in the direction of your vision.

Bonus Tip: Once you determine your objectives, it's a good idea to look at them monthly and give them a hard look at the end of each quarter. However, you have to give them time to work, so it's important not to change them too frequently. Your strategies are where you can adjust to ensure that you are meeting your objectives.

THE SWOT ANALYSIS: DETERMINING YOUR RESOURCES

Now that you've thought more deeply about your business plan, it's useful to perform a SWOT analysis. I know, it sounds sort of official and maybe a little intimidating, but it's easy and important. I'll break it down.

SWOT stands for **Strengths, Weaknesses, Opportunities, Threats**. In the context of our objectives, we look at the SWOT to determine why we aren't already accomplishing our objectives and what we can use to accomplish them. This is a simple exercise—just put down what comes to mind. Something that can help you think in these terms is to consider that strengths and weaknesses usually come from *within* the office or team and opportunities and threats usually come from *the external environment*.

Strengths

Consider these elements and think of them in terms of what the team has already that can be leveraged even more to help achieve your objectives:

- experience in the industry
- dynamics of your team
- qualities of your team members
- relationships

Weaknesses

A word of warning: in my experience of coaching business leaders and their teams, I've seen that there is a tendency to identify many weaknesses. In other words, people are good at seeing where they are weak but not as skilled at identifying their strengths. It's useful to review the team's weaknesses (remember blind spots?) because it helps you think through strategies and tactics for improvement, but it's more important to focus on leveraging strengths because that is where you will see the *most* progress toward your objectives.

Consider the following:

- how you spend your time
- dynamics of your team
- level of experience
- how your vision, mission, and core values are shared and communicated

Opportunities

Write down how you

- form new relationships,
- improve or expand existing relationships,
- launch new product offerings, and
- develop a niche—that is, how you can differentiate yourself from everyone else in the market.

Of course, there are many opportunities out there; the key is to make sure you are pursuing opportunities that align with your vision, mission, and core values.

Threats

It's fine to jot down everything that comes to mind, but try to focus on the things you can actually influence. For example, if there is a new federal regulation that poses a threat, feel free to record it, but don't dwell on it if you can't change it. It's more useful to consider how you'll respond to that change. Something like increased competition is very helpful to consider in depth, because you can spend time brainstorming with your team about how to better differentiate yourself.

If this all makes sense, then you're ready to do your SWOT analysis. Feel free to photocopy it or download it from my website. Remember, this is a brainstorming activity that will help you decide on strategies and tactics to achieve your objectives.

Complete the SWOT analysis by thinking through the areas that already set you up for success and those that may impact future opportunities. Generally, strengths/weaknesses are internal factors and opportunities/threats are external factors.

Strengths	Weaknesses
Opportunities	**Threats**

IDENTIFYING STRATEGIES THAT
ILLUMINATE YOUR VISION

Now that you've identified your objectives and performed your SWOT analysis, it's time to start developing strategies. When we talk strategy, we are talking about developing a big picture view of how you will accomplish your objectives—that is, how you will overcome your weaknesses and capitalize on your strengths. When you think about the big picture, it's helpful to think of it in these terms:

1. How am I going to accomplish my objectives?
2. Who is going to accomplish these objectives?
3. What do I need to accomplish these objectives?

Let's talk about how this might look. You've done your SWOT analysis, and one thing you've determined is that you have a person on your team who is not very experienced in sales. To address that, you need to identify a strategy to overcome that weakness.

Your strategy could look like this: **Provide sales training to the individual, over the course of the year, around the services and products we offer.**

Maybe another weakness you've identified is with your own personal management style. Perhaps you struggle with holding people accountable and haven't clearly identified what their role is. As a result, your team members may not be sure how they can be "successful," since that hasn't been defined and doesn't seem to be "required." In this case, your strategy could look like this: **Clearly identify team member expectations and implement a system for holding people accountable to those expectations.**

Let's get specific to capitalizing on strengths to overcome weaknesses.

Strength: A team member, Kaily, is exceptional at life insurance sales. She also spends a lot of time doing service work.

Strategy: Take some of the service workload off of Kaily and let her focus almost exclusively on life sales for the rest of the year.

> It's important to remember that calling something a weakness is not about blaming the person without the experience. It's a team weakness, and to overcome it, we must support the person in getting the experience they need.

Now let's think about threats for a minute and how you could identify strategies in relation to identified threats.

Threat: There is increased competition.

Strategy: Use the opportunity to differentiate yourself from the competition. Based on the personalities you have in your office, identify what you are most passionate about or where your niche market is. Maybe you want to focus on financial services planning for small businesses because you have a lot of experience there and can relate to the business owner who knows they "should" be doing that but is overwhelmed. Maybe there is a type of client you care the most about, like middle-aged couples with children. Once you identify that niche, passion, and target, work to develop yourselves more in that direction.

How Many Strategies Do You Need?

It's easy to get carried away when you start thinking about strategies, and this is when it is important to go back to your one-page business plan. You don't need 12 strategies. In fact, you don't want 12, because without focus, you won't accomplish them. You just need 2–3 strategies that align with your **most** important objectives and are based on what you identified in your SWOT analysis. Two to three strategies for the next quarter, that's all. And hey, if one is significant enough, you can just focus on that one. That's absolutely fine. In my work, I've seen that most business leaders do really well with just 2–3.

When you hone in on those few strategies, you will feel a renewed sense of focus and excitement because you'll easily see how you can make progress toward your vision. You'll be focused and on fire!

TACTICS: BREATHING LIFE INTO YOUR BUSINESS PLAN

We've spent a lot of time talking about the different elements that help you accomplish your vision as a leader. By now, you're probably ready to just get moving. That's why tactics are so great. Because they allow us to set things in motion and on the trajectory we want. Be sure you're climbing the right ladder!

Strategies versus Tactics

It's easy to confuse the two! One way to think about it is this:

A strategy is the mental process of thinking through how we'll achieve our objectives, our overall direction, and focus.

Tactics are the day-by-day activities that we commit to doing in order to achieve our objectives.

How to Develop Tactics

The problem with monthly sales goals is they are **lagging results**; by the time you get to the end of the month, it's too late to impact the goal. Instead, think through each step on the way to sales and drill down to the daily activities that drive your results. These activities should be within a team member's control and be predictive of results. Those are called **leading indicators**.

Your goal is to look at your objectives and strategies and think how you can become very specific in your approach to them, so that your team members know very clearly what is expected of them, hour by hour, day by day. It's frustrating for them if they're not clear, they do their best, and you're not happy!

Let's assume one of your strategies is to clearly identify team expectations. That strategy is based, in part, on one of your identified team objectives:

Sell 10 life insurance policies a month, for example.

What activities or tactics will drive the accomplishment of that objective? The answer identifies what specific action you need to be doing, not the result you're looking for. Let's think it through.

How many appointments does it take to sell one life insurance policy? (You can determine this by thinking through your prior experiences and making your best guess, based on calculations.)

Say it takes five appointments to make one sale.

Now ask how many phone calls it takes to schedule an appointment.

If it takes 10 calls to schedule an appointment, do the math and learn that

50 calls per month = 1 policy sold

Remember, that's just for one policy, though, so look at the numbers for 10 policies per month:

# of policies per month: 10
# of appointments to sell 10 policies: 50
# of calls to make 50 appointments: 500

Wow, that sounds like a lot. But let's break it down more.

If you divide that by 20 working days in a month, that's 25 calls per day. Then divide it by the number of team members you have (say you have four), that's 6.25 calls per person, per day.

Now you have a very specific daily expectation to communicate to your team. In fact, walk your team through this exercise. Then they can see how every phone call, cross-sell, and upsell is a step on their way to success.

Use my Activity Calculator to identify your key tactics. It looks more complicated than it really is! The first section shows sample activity needed to generate 10 life policies.

Goal = _____ *Life Policies a Month Placed*		
How many life policies do I need to sell to have _____ stay on the books?		Sales needed: _____
How many appointments does it take to sell one life policy?		Appointments: _____
Appointments: _____ ×	Monthly goal: _____	Appts per month: _____
What percentage of appointments show up?		_____%
Percentage that show up divided by appointments desired:		__./.__ = __ scheduled appointments needed
How many "asks" to get one life or insurance review appointment?		"Asks" needed: _____
"Asks"/Appt Ratio: _____ ×	Monthly Appt Goal: _____	"Asks" needed: _____
"Asks" needed ÷ 20 days a month	_____ ÷ 20 =	_____ "asks" a day
"Asks" a day ÷ # of team members	_____ ÷ _____ =	_____ "asks" a day per team member

Goal = ___10___ *Life Policies a Month Placed*		
How many life policies do I need to sell to have **10** stay on the books?		Sales needed: **13**
How many appointments does it take to sell one life policy?		Appointments: **5**
Appointments: **5** ×	Monthly goal: **13**	Appts per month: **65**
What percentage of appointments show up?		75%
Percentage that show up divided by appointments desired:		**65** / **.75** = **87** scheduled appointments needed
How many "asks" to get one life or insurance review appointment?		"Asks" needed: **10**
"Asks"/Appt Ratio: **10** ×	Monthly Appt Goal: **87**	"Asks" needed: **870**
"Asks" needed ÷ 20 days a month	**870** ÷ 20 =	**44** "asks" a day
"Asks" a day ÷ # of team members	**44** ÷ **3** =	**15** "asks" a day per team member
"Asks" = pivots and/or calling prospects to ask for an appointment Appts = Appointments Now create your own customized version of this table!		

You can take this same concept and apply it to anything you want to sell for your business success; in fact, this idea of drilling down to daily activities that drive results can usually be identified for any area of business you want to focus on.

Stay on Course

I see it in my work regularly: leaders are bombarded with so many cool business resources that present numerous great ideas, but if you went after all those ideas, you'd never get anything done! Why? Because you'd constantly be changing directions.

The most success comes from *identifying specific tactics* with team members and *making them easy for the team to do consistently over time*.

"What's easy to do, is also easy to not do." —Jim Rohn

We all know how easy it is to be busy, but *we are often busy doing the wrong things*. One of the best ways to focus on the most important things (like sales) every day, regardless of what else is going on, is by implementing another tactic—one that serves as a mechanism for tracking progress and holding each person accountable. If you learn to track the simple activities that team members will be doing, you will learn how to help them be successful. Start by using my Tracking Tool on page 55.

It's Alive!

As with your business plan, your tactics are living and breathing; you can identify and implement them, and you will **learn as you go** which activities and how many of them really drive the results you are seeking.

You will probably find that you need to tweak them moving forward. You can do that as part of your weekly and monthly planning activities. That's where the Tracking Tool will come in handy—to inform that discussion. And don't forget: your tactics should serve the strategies you've developed, which in turn, serve your objectives and, ultimately, your mission and vision.

I've given you the Tracking Tool to start thinking about how you can check in on progress, but we'll also talk more specifically about *how* to do that—that is, how to ensure consistency and proper tactical execution (yes, I just wrote, "tactical execution").

Weekly Activity Tracking Log

Name: _____

For Week of: _____

—Activity—

	Monday	Tuesday	Wednesday	Thursday	Friday	Goal
Calls to schedule Insurance Reviews (__ a day)						
Pivots (__ a day) to XYZ products						
Pivots to XYZ products (__ a day)						
Goal						

—Results—

	Monday	Tuesday	Wednesday	Thursday	Friday
Reviews Scheduled					
Life Applications					
Other Applications					

Individual Team Member Expectations: _____ Sales Contacts a day discussing

_____

This can be accomplished through outgoing phone calls and/or pivots during conversations with customers.

Office Production Goals:

_____ "Kept" Appointments per week per team member/20 scheduled

Life: _____ Issued per month

Other product goals: _____

Section 4:

Focus Your Time

Chapter 11

High-Leverage Activities
Drive Results

One of the best ways to live strengths-based leadership is by identifying which 2–3 areas investing your time in would have the biggest ripple effect on your business. If you *focus on activities that leverage your strengths effectively in those areas*, you will have a lasting, powerful effect on your business and your team. Simply put, we are talking about high-leverage activities.

WHAT IS A HIGH-LEVERAGE ACTIVITY?

Think of it this way: You can be pretty successful just by working hard. But at some point, just working hard doesn't work, because *what* you are working hard at is what determines your success.

Sure, you can spend a lot of time on responding to requests; those may feel like high-leverage activities, but they're probably not.

When you think about high-leverage activities, it's helpful to keep this question in mind: *Do they help you, as a leader, get results through others?*

High-leverage activities often fall into the following realms:

- building the team
- strategic planning
- marketing

But which activities are high-leverage is different for everyone. One of the best ways to identify your own high-leverage activities is to do the following simple exercise.

Directions
1. List everything you do.
2. Transfer activities you are great at, love doing, and that are high-impact to appropriate columns. Add high-impact activities you'd like to do but aren't doing that would make a big impact on your results.
3. For activities you don't love doing or aren't great at, can you apply one of the three *D*s (Delete, Delegate, Defer)?

Four-Column Exercise

Credited to Larry Broughton/Broughton Advisory

"Just because I can, doesn't mean I should." —Phil Dyer

Everything I Do	What I'm Great At	What I Love Doing	High Impact

This can really help you get a grasp on what you are doing and where you can spend your time more effectively (i.e., focus on high-leverage activities). Some activities just don't need to be done, others don't need to be done right now, and still others can be done better by someone other than yourself.

To help with this shift in mind-set, think about how you value your time. Say you are an insurance agent bringing in $3 million in premiums annually. Divide that by 2,080 work hours in a year. That's about $1,400 an hour. You need to look at all the activities you are currently doing and ask yourself, *Would I pay someone that much to do that task?*

If not, then you need to decide whom on your team you can delegate those activities to and which activities are worth that much to you (i.e., high-leverage activities).

MAKING HIGH-LEVERAGE ACTIVITIES PART OF THE TEAM

Just as with identifying strengths, high-leverage activities are most effective when you've identified them for yourself first. When you get a grasp on how to best spend your own time—working *on* the business instead of *in* the business—then you can start helping your team members determine their own high-leverage activities. This is where individual strengths and effective delegation come together to create a highly engaged and productive team. Ask your team members to do the Four-Column Exercise too, and then compare their results with yours to hone in on the team's true, high-leverage activities.

CHAPTER 12

The Four Hats of a Business Leader

In prior chapters, we discussed developing your plan and shared a little about leadership. Let's talk more about leadership from the context of the roles that you fill as a business owner.

WEARING MANY HATS

When you first thought about starting a business, you most likely realized you'd be wearing many hats. There are four distinct hats that most owners have in common and they are that of the

- leader,
- manager,
- mentor, and
- coach.

It's important, when thinking about these four hats (or roles), to realize that **each requires a different set of talents**. Let's start by looking more closely at leading and managing a high-performing business, and we'll talk about mentoring and coaching in the next section.

Leadership Hat

- big-picture perspective
- setting the direction for the business/strategic planning
- having the vision about what the company is, where it is going, and communicating these
- sensing and understanding changes in the environment locally and industry wide
- inspiring/influencing others
- leading from the front and propelling people in the direction you want to go

Essentially, leadership requires that you always have an eye on fulfilling your vision, a clear picture of the environment, and the ability to explain how day-to-day activities fuel personal and organizational success. Leadership is also about setting an example of conduct for your team and creating a productive and motivating work atmosphere.

Management Hat

- structure and clarify team expectations
- hold team members accountable
- manage team activities
- direct individual behavior toward organizational results
- align and focus resources to achieve goals

At its best, managing is about bringing out the best results from people and getting organizational results. Part of the role of managing is setting boundaries. For instance, *What time does everyone need to show up for work? How do you want them to respond to customer complaints? What specific results do you expect from employees?*

Ideally, though, management focus should be on continually thinking, *How do I consistently bring out the best in that person?*

SET CLEAR RULES AND EXPECTATIONS FROM THE GET-GO

Start by identifying the actions or lack of action that will cost employees their job. Put those in writing. Then identify the expectations that need to be met. Put those in writing. Be sure these are communicated often and have your employees describe them back to you in their own words, to make sure they understand. Don't assume they understand. Review these on a regular schedule.

Once you set clear rules and people understand that staying within those parameters is job security, it's important to clearly state what level of performance is required. Be specific in promising, and consistent in delivering, consequences—including rewards and recognition. If rules are broken or expectations aren't met, you **must** have a series of counseling discussions to help the person excel at their job. Otherwise, you're "hoping," not "managing," and you're unwittingly letting your vision be held captive by your employees! That's not what they signed up for—most people **want** to do a good job. When performance expectations are clear and specific, people know what they need to do and can feel secure in their work, as long as they are meeting those rules and expectations. I'm assuming you're providing all the resources they need in order to do their job. When all of this is in place, they feel a lot more comfortable going "above and beyond the call of duty."

You can always add to your written rules and expectations and alter them, but you need to start somewhere. We tend to avoid this step, because no one wants to think about things not working out. The irony is that if you do think about them, write them down, and communicate them, your chances of success increase tenfold.

Gallup's 30+ years of research proves that a fundamental need of all employees is a clear understanding of what's expected of them at work. Yet only half of the employees they surveyed have clarity on what's expected of them. No wonder people are stressed!

When I think about management—setting boundaries and expectations— I am reminded of a Ken Blanchard quote: **"A river without banks is just a puddle."**

Think about all the energy in a river that is built by water being forced through the walls/banks of the river. If we were to dig away at those banks, the energy in the water would wane and lose power. As managers, when we establish clear boundaries, we help people focus their energy. That's a good thing!

As you can see, it's essential for you to be able to switch hats . . . well, at the drop of a hat. Think about this in terms of *what your employees need most from you* at a particular time **or** *what your business needs most for you to focus on* in a particular moment. That's why having your mission, vision, and expectations in place is so important. They compose the foundation that enables you to see what roles need to be filled and when.

CHAPTER 13

The Distinction between Mentoring and Coaching

Continuing our discussion of the four hats a leader must wear, let's look at the distinction between mentoring and coaching in a business. In simple terms, mentoring is about providing support and guidance based on your own experiences, whereas coaching is helping people identify their own objectives, partnering with them to identify alternatives, and creating internal change.

MENTORING

Laurent Daloz, in his book *Mentor*, describes three crucial roles mentors play:

- provide support
- challenge people
- help people find their vision

We provide support as a mentor whenever we let people know that they're in a safe environment to try to do their job. Some people get overwhelmed when they're new to an industry because there are so many complexities. They're hesitant to even attempt a sales conversation with a prospect because they think they don't know enough.

As a mentor, you might start by saying, "That's totally understand-able." Then you would share your own knowledge/experiences to help shortcut the learning process for that person. You do this to give moti-vated people something to run with. Show them the path and make it safe for them to jump. It's a little different with people who are unmo-tivated or who lack confidence, and we'll talk about that in a minute.

As a mentor, you also help new team members become integrated with and adapted to the work environment. You might introduce them to other team members and say something like "Hey Ron, would you sit with Cliff for a couple of hours? Cliff, watch Ron, he's a great self-starter and has good intuition."

In this way, you are giving new team members the opportunity to learn methods that work, and you are enabling other team members to act as mentors and to build their own self-esteem and experience.

Mentoring is first about providing support, but equally important, it's about providing challenge. Challenge is a key part of mentoring be-cause that is where growth comes in. Essentially, when support is high but challenge is low, people feel good about themselves, but they won't grow very much. This doesn't mean you need to inundate them with challenges. It means that people thrive with a balance of challenge and support. It works the other way too. If challenge is really high and sup-port is really low, you won't see growth either. They'll keep their heads low and try not to rock the boat.

Helping people find their vision is one of the most rewarding aspects of mentoring. You get to ask your employees about what excites them in their work. They get to tell you what their dream is for the work they are doing—whether gaining 500 new clients by the end of the year or selling six life insurance policies. The key is to do visioning exercises with them and help them paint a picture of their individual success in the framework of the business' vision and mission. Ask them what steps will get them there *and what kind of person they need to be* to get there. Ask them what support they need from you. It might be entirely differ-ent than what you were thinking. When this picture is clear, the team member is more likely to achieve success and you have a better sense of how you can best help them.

COACHING

The International Coach Federation defines coaching as ***"Partnering with clients in a thought-provoking and creative process that inspires them to maximize their personal and professional potential."***

Gallup likes to remind strengths coaches that coaching occurs in the passenger seat, not the driver's seat. Done right, the coaching process is about asking a lot of questions, holding up a mirror to them, and helping them find their own way to develop their potential. This is significantly different from mentors sharing their knowledge and experience as a way to help others move forward.

Coaching is about helping people see themselves in a different way, often for the first time. It is rare that any of us have people in our lives that can help us really see ourselves objectively.

Keep this in mind: If you find yourself asking a lot of questions, deeply listening, and reflecting back answers and observations to your protégé, you are probably coaching. If you find yourself sharing your experiences and best practices of what's worked for you in the past, you are probably mentoring.

In your role as a business leader, you will be doing both. The key is to know how to weave **both** into conversations with your team members. With newer team members, you'll most likely find yourself spending most of your time as a mentor helping them learn the skills of the craft. However, there are a lot of opportunities for coaching. For instance, asking team members to share past success stories with you is a great coaching opportunity. As you help them explore their own past successes, ask questions to help them see why and how they were successful. Then ask how they can apply those same abilities to their current challenges. You'll learn a lot about your employees this way too.

A couple of clues on when to switch between coaching and mentoring: If it's a skill or knowledge issue on something that's new, mentoring and training are usually called for. You'll be sharing best practices, educating, and shortening the learning curve for your team member. However, if an employee knows what needs to be done, but isn't doing it successfully or there is a confidence issue, a coaching approach is most helpful. Be sure you're asking mostly open-ended "what" and "how" questions. Use "why" questions sparingly, as they can feel accusatory or judgmental. A key is to be truly curious as you help them figure out what is going on. Don't ask leading questions, because even if they start with "I don't know," they really *do* know. Just keep asking in a caring manner.

There are a lot of elements to successful coaching and mentoring. A good place to start is to ask yourself these questions: *Is there something I should share with them?* or *Is there something I should ask them?*

CHAPTER 14

Feeding the Flame:
Become a Talent Connoisseur

A good leader, manager, or coach can help someone who's very talented become an outstanding team member. But if that person just doesn't have the talent needed for the type of job that you're looking to fill, it can result in struggle and frustration for everybody. That's why the most important decisions that you make as a leader have to do with selecting who will be on your team. Essentially, you must become a "talent connoisseur."

TALENT VERSUS EXPERIENCE

I touched on this earlier when we talked about Jim Collins's notion of getting the right people in the right seats on the bus. When we think about filling roles on our team, we tend to think in terms of finding people who have experience in the field. As it turns out, that is not always the best idea. Why? Because we can train almost anyone to do a job, but *it's very difficult to teach someone to be motivated*. People are naturally motivated to do the things they were born with talent to do. They're not intrinsically motivated to do things that are a struggle for them. Either they have motivation to do a certain job or they don't. Excelling at a job requires a certain level of talent. As Gallup points out, we can train for skills and knowledge, but we can't train talent. Instead, it's helpful to look for those who have the talent and the drive to be successful at that role.

How Do You Become a Talent Connoisseur?

1. **Start with your highest performing coworkers and employees.**
   It helps to make a list of those on your team and those whom you've worked with in the past who are/were highly successful at their job.

2. **Interview them.**
   One of the best ways to understand talent and motivation is to ask your successful peers pointed questions about how they do what they do and how their team members function. You want to get a clear idea of what makes talented people tick in your environment.
   - How do they approach each customer or sale?
   - When they call their first customer, what is their goal and how do they achieve it?
   - What motivates them to pick up that phone and call people?
   - Where else have they experienced success in their life and what was their secret to it?

3. **Develop character sketches.**
   As you learn about what works for others, you can start developing a picture of the types of talents, tactics, and behaviors that work well for the positions you want to fill. Create a list of the attributes for success in that position.

4. **Develop a talent strategy.**
   Once you have an idea of the kind talent and drive you're looking for, it's time to develop a strategy:
   - Create a talent file that helps you track interactions with potential employees.
   - Always be scouting for the next employee, wherever you are, regardless of whether you are ready to hire someone or not.
   - Think about hiring the same way you think about marketing and selling products. Your effort must be **constant**, even if you are only in the planning stages of opening your own business.

- Ask your team members who they know that would excel as a team member. Who would they like to work with? Why?

5. **Employ regular talent-scouting tactics.**
   - Have at least one or two coffee meetings a month with an "employee prospect." Think outside the box! An employee prospect could be the person at the coffee shop who always upsells you the muffin you didn't know you wanted.
   - If you aren't part of a networking group, join one! There are always talented folks to meet there. If they aren't necessarily a fit for your business or the role you are looking to fill, they will likely know someone who is.
   - Ask every potential employee the same questions that you've asked your successful coworkers and employees. Make a note of the stories they tell about selling the most Girl Scout cookies as a kid or more raffle tickets than anyone else. When you hear people repeat patterns of success, it's a strong clue that they could be the type of talent you are looking for in your business.
   - Keep track of the talented people you've had coffee with and keep in touch. Celebrate the successes that they are having.

By the time you are ready to hire, you will have a wealth of potentials to work with! There is no need to "post and pray." Instead, you have a deliberate list of candidates already. You've become a "talent connoisseur" who has scouted purposefully over time and developed relationships that are poised to flourish.

Section 5:

Focus Your Team's Time

CHAPTER 15

The Burn of the Production Curve

As with most things in life, business ebbs and flows; yet you have more power to control the impacts of those ups and downs than you think you do. Methods that contribute to this include the following:

- consistency
- attentiveness
- accountability
- after-action reviews

When you get really busy and production is rocking, it's important to stay focused on the small things that, if done daily, drive results. The most common problem arises when team members get so busy that they reduce their number of sales/marketing activities in order to keep up with service work from new sales.

Think about this scenario as an example: An insurance agency is extremely busy processing applications because they've been consistently doing the activities that drive sales. That's a good problem to have! However, would the team be comfortable approaching you with the following conversation?

Man, I processed 100 applications last month and I'm on track to do 110 this month, but I'm getting so many requests from underwriting that either I need to figure out some way of having these taken care of elsewhere, or I need to lower the number of outbound calls I'm making, which is going to lower my sales volume. What do you think?

If you're not proactive about this, sales activity will start slowing down, which eventually will affect your results. Hopefully, you will have created an environment where your employees feel completely comfortable bringing a "problem" of this type to you. This is a great open conversation to have. So together you strategize, and it's really fun. But how can you address that wonderful problem before it occurs?

STAY ALERT TO THE BURN OF THE PRODUCTION CURVE

Take a look at the next image; imagine your team completing all the leading activities identified in earlier chapters and then reducing those activities as they get busy. How will that impact your results 4–8 weeks down the road?

The key is to never let go of production-driving activities.

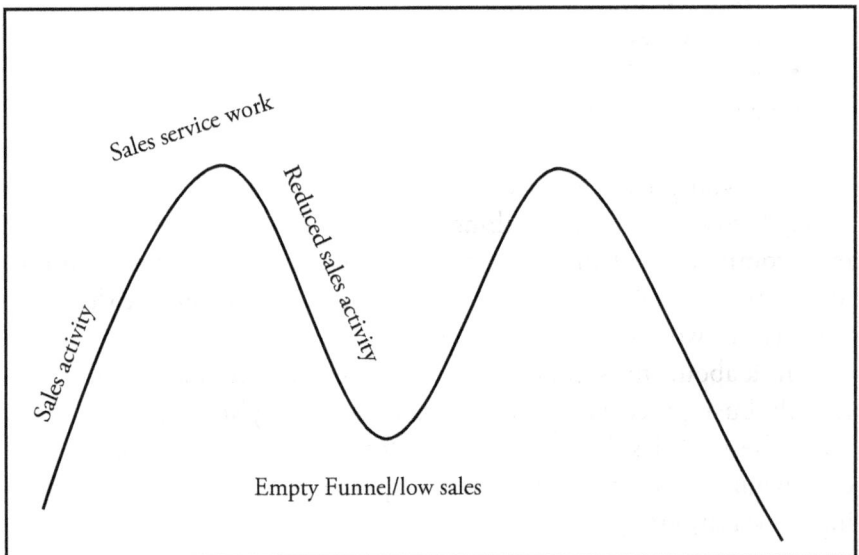

NEVER LET GO OF PRODUCTION-DRIVING ACTIVITIES

I realize that at times, you may need to let go of production-driving activities, at least somewhat, but when you do, it should be a conscious choice. Having that consciousness makes it *very clear what the consequences are* so that you are constantly thinking of ways to minimize the impacts of letting go of those activities. Stephen Covey said, ***"When you pick up one end of a stick, you pick up the other end."***

Essentially, *all action or lack of action has a consequence somewhere down the road.* It's not always a bad thing, it's just important for you to be aware of the ramifications of your daily actions. If you don't hit your numbers on Monday or Tuesday, you still have the ability to correct your week, but by Friday, there's not a whole lot you can do about meeting your quota for the week.

Keep *both* ends of the stick constantly in mind as you travel across the peaks and valleys!

CHAPTER 16

Fire Control: Attention to Daily Results

We've already done a lot of work planning for success in our businesses. We've also revisited why it is we are doing all this. Now is a good time to review the foundation of the planning process in order to prepare yourself for the next step: *attentiveness*.

When you take the time to (1) create the foundation of clear vision, mission, and objectives for your business and (2) track your activity at least weekly, your long-term results should not be a surprise. Identifying and tracking your numbers tells you exactly what you are shooting for and how close you are getting to those targets.

Sounds easy, right? You're probably thinking that it *isn't* as easy as it sounds because there are so many things coming at you, such as

- requests from other people,
- requests from your company, and
- all sorts of things that you continually need to respond to.

It is so easy to get focused on what other people ask of you and *not* focus on doing what is most important to drive forward to your goals.

IT'S TIME TO BE ATTENTIVE

I am not implying that you aren't already attentive, but *are you attentive to the right things?*

If you aren't paying attention, weeks go by and then months, where you're just busy doing a lot of things that aren't high-priority activities.

Once you have that crystal-clear picture of what drives your success, you have three to five activities (phone calls, cross-sells, upsells, pivots, etc.) that you *know* you should focus on each day consistently. Those three to five things are the key to moving forward.

In truth, every night you can tell if you did the most important things to drive your success that day. Occasionally, you won't do them all or maybe any of them. That's OK if that's the exception, not the rule. Once *you* hit your stride with this, you will be able to help your team members hold themselves accountable in the same way.

BEING ATTENTIVE IS CHECKING IN

Remember, the purpose of that one-page business plan is to have something that you can keep at the forefront of people's minds (including your own). Basically, it creates a structure and builds the systems that are designed to focus your efforts around what you're trying to achieve.

The first part, of course, is to design the plan, but *no plan survives contact with the real world*. Or at least, it doesn't stay fully intact.

What? An airplane is never really 100% on track; there needs to be *constant correction* for wind and other factors. It's useful to think about this in terms of your business plan; once you have that plan and an accountability system in place, you need to be diligent about checking in with your team members regularly.

HOW CAN YOU BE ATTENTIVE?

- Once you have established a way to check in with *yourself* daily, begin checking in with your employees at least once a week. That way you can get a gauge of how they are doing and what challenges they've run across before it's too late. They'll feel good about getting your helpful (not critical) attention, so they'll be more engaged in their work too.

- When you make this a habit, then it's not a surprise to them if you check in on their activities, even daily, if that's proven necessary.
- Monthly, you should be looking at the results and then comparing your strategies to the results, because sometimes you have to tweak the strategies to achieve the results you are looking for.

THE BENEFITS OF BEING ATTENTIVE

- Once it's crystal clear in everybody's mind what the required activities are, then you can celebrate successes or make corrections and coach if people aren't hitting their numbers.
- Sometimes attentiveness helps you identify systemic problems. For example, perhaps the team gets overloaded. If you're not checking in, you go along happily, thinking that everybody's making 10 calls a week to schedule appointments (for example), when really, half the team is overloaded with service work. The consequence will show up when you look at your weekly production reports, so check in at least weekly.

If there's a results gap, there is usually an activity gap. By checking in, you can quickly see where you're not quite hitting the numbers, and you can increase or adjust the level of activity to get the results you want.

CHAPTER 17

How Meetings Support Your Tactics . . . and Your Success!

It's all well and good to identify the tactics that will help you succeed and the day-to-day methods for tracking. In fact, it's necessary. But how do you, as a team, stay on task? With meetings, of course. I know, you're probably thinking, "Meetings are a joke!" Or at least, you've thought that once or twice in your life. That's often because meetings aren't productive or designed well. It's not the idea of the meeting that is broken. It's the execution.

When we learn how to execute meetings properly, we not only help our team stay on task but also build synergy, motivate each other, and develop open communication—all qualities of an engaged, productive team.

THE MEETING FRAMEWORK

Patrick Lencioni describes a great process for having team meetings in his book *Death by Meeting*. There are two types that are really crucial.

The Daily Standup Meeting: Pick a time to meet at the beginning of each day. The idea is that people won't ramble on endlessly, because everybody's standing up—they're antsy to get to work. Everybody says what they're going to do that day to further drive toward the goals. For example, someone might say, "I'm going to be making 10 calls today and I've got three appointments lined up. One appointment might be a little bit long, so can I get a little support covering the phone?" It's an opportunity to quickly hit on opportunities and challenges that may come up that day. It shouldn't take any longer than 10 minutes.

Weekly Strategy Meeting: It's very important to have a meeting where you compare tactical activities. Look at the number of tactical activities that people committed to, *compare them to how many were actually done*, and then discuss results. A great approach for this comes from a book called *The Four Disciplines of Execution* by Chris McChesney and Sean Covey.

During the meeting, your team members should address each of the following four areas:

1. What they did throughout the week
2. The results they got
3. What they learned
4. What they will do next week

Essentially, a weekly strategy meeting opens the door to conversations about how to address challenges. For example, say people committed to doing 20 phone calls a day, and they only did two a day for the last week. You can talk about what happened. Maybe there's some sort of systemic problem within the business that is overloading people with detail work. This meeting also enables you to see where you are making progress and celebrate that.

IN THE BEGINNING

In order to maximize the benefit of your team meetings, it's helpful to set the foundation with each team member. We do that by spending time one-on-one beforehand, discussing the one-page business plan, the goals and why they are important, and how that team member is expected to contribute specifically. You can't effectively engage your team if **each** person doesn't understand the key objectives of the business and how they are to make their contribution to achieving those objectives.

Encourage them to ask themselves, *What are the key tasks that I do every day, to contribute my part to achieving our objectives?*

These can include cross-selling during client calls and meetings, scheduling comprehensive reviews with existing clients, or reaching out to potential clients.

Leaders are usually good at identifying a multitude of activities that drive results and are within the team member's control. The key is to make a distinction between leading and lagging activities.

THE DIFFERENCE BETWEEN LEADING AND LAGGING

When you look at your objectives, numerous activities contribute to accomplishing them. Yet it's important to recognize which are more directly *predictive* of results. For example, say you're an insurance agent who wants to sell 75 applications a month. You can't predict who will buy and who will not. If you are nearing the end of your month and you've only sold 20, there is not much you can do about it. That "sold" number is a lagging indicator.

However, when you know how many calls, *on average*, it takes to make a sale, you can apply that to your activities. The number of outbound calls is something that is always within your influence and predictive of results. Having made 50 calls this week is a leading indicator, because whether or not a customer says "yes" or "no" isn't in your control, but if you call enough customers, the sales will take care of themselves. If a team member only made 10 calls each week for the last three months, because you've been talking to them about it already, they shouldn't be surprised if there is a consequence.

When you (1) are deliberate about the structure of your meetings, (2) keep a focus on leading activities, and (3) hold people accountable, you are sure to see results! Too many business owners don't take the time to determine or track leading activities, or they do but don't feel comfortable holding people accountable. Then they wonder why they're not doing better, or they get frustrated when they miss out on that sales incentive trip!

CHAPTER 18

The Traffic Light: Measuring Your Daily Success

Another way to be attentive, track your activities, and lead from your strengths is by using the *traffic light concept*. I first read about this traffic-signal concept in *The Ownership Quotient*, where the authors described the process Victoria's Secret uses to compare sales results with sales targets daily (sometimes every two hours!). In my work, I've found that using a "traffic light" as the daily and weekly gauge for team and leader success helps keep the focus on key priorities.

HOW DOES IT WORK?

It's a simple concept, which is nice. We don't need to make things complicated! The traffic light gives everyone a simple and clear indication of how well they met their daily or weekly metrics. A green light means that you met all your metrics for the day (or ultimately the week), a yellow light tells you that you did OK, but there was room for improvement, and a red light tells you that the day got away from you (you didn't hit any of your metrics) and tomorrow you'll need to double your efforts.

Let's relish in the feeling of a green light day for a second. You look at your list of targeted leading activities. Today, you made all 15 outbound phone calls, you accomplished all five cross-sells during incoming calls, you made one upsell, and you asked for referrals from five customers. It's a green light day!

Traffic lights help you keep a real focus on your identified tactics/activities. This is important because *we know, for a fact, that when people focus on consistent, systematic activities (doing them over and over again), we see results.* Traffic lights ensure that you are getting results from things that are in your control. That's when it gets really fun. Why? Because you actually begin to realize that you **can** control your own destiny. Traffic lights help give you awareness of what it takes to reach your goals: consistency and focus on the few activities that are *most* important to reach your goals. Focusing on these numbers **keeps you focused on what's important to you versus what's important to other people**. It's only fair to keep a balance, right?

HOW DAILY SUCCESS TRANSFORMS DECEMBER

I would guess you typically dread December. You're nearing your deadline and the goal you set for yourself. Often when December arrives, you're frantically trying to make up for lost time, and you waste time thinking of all the things you "should have" done.

In my experience, business owners often find themselves scrambling to make their numbers in December. That's no fun! December should be about planning the following year and then enjoying the holidays. When you focus on your traffic lights throughout the year, you always know exactly what milepost you've reached and you're confident you'll meet your goal early. This brings us to one of my favorite philosophies: ***Don't make your numbers in December. Make December a celebration of your numbers!***

The idea is that when you plan, pay attention, and focus on your daily successes, the year takes care of itself. When you don't plan, pay attention, and focus, time just becomes a big blur of *trying to keep up*. That's stressful and hard on relationships. December *can* be a celebration, not a scramble. Sure, there will be times when you hit the numbers and want to go even higher, but December should always be a celebration.

VISUALIZE DAILY SUCCESS

The additional benefit of traffic lights is that they make it easy for us to have a visual reminder of where we are. That visual allows you to know right away whether you are falling behind or getting ahead. There are numerous goal-tracking graphs available online that you can employ as a visual reminder.

Remember, as you're contemplating which visual to use, be sure to pull on your team strengths. It's ideal to have a visual graph that means something to the entire team, so utilize your team's strengths when you create your visual signs/reports.

Section 6:

Engage Your Team

CHAPTER 19

Four Keys to Extraordinary Employee Performance

Let's talk more about how having clear expectations is important for employee engagement. To increase employee performance, you have to be able to answer these four questions:

1. Do they know what to do?
2. Do they know how to do it?
3. Are the confident in their ability to do it?
4. Are they willing to do it?

This amounts to four very different conversations.

1. DO EMPLOYEES KNOW WHAT TO DO?

When you think about opening your office or forming your team, think through the fundamental expectations that each employee will need to fulfill:

- Define roles clearly and specifically, segmented into various specialties, with sharp objectives tied to that role. Talk them over with the person as soon as they are hired, and get them to tell them back to you. Have a deep conversation so the person can ask questions and get clarity. You cannot spend too much time on this! Encourage them to ask for help if they feel themselves getting pulled by conflicting priorities. Asking for help should be encouraged regularly if you want to create a highly motivated team.

- Repeat your performance expectations in regular meetings with employees to ensure they are really clear. Ensure your employees know you will hold them accountable.
- Develop systems and structures that the whole office understands and that create accountability. **Publish** statistics for each person and the team as a whole, so everyone on the team can see them, just like they do in sports. See the book *The Game of Work* by Charles A. Coonradt for some examples on charts that show expectations versus each person's performance. He proposes we should enjoy work as much as we do play! Many offices post these in their coffee room. Have fun contests.
- Follow through with recognition, rewards, and consequences *consistently*.

This is a huge foundational piece for employee engagement. Everybody assumes that it's clear what a person in a particular job should be doing, but in fact, it's rarely that clear. When I ask business leaders if their team members know what to do, the answer is always a confident "yes." When I ask team members the same question, most of the time I get a lot of hemming and hawing and a lot of tentative guesses. *I'm often reminded of a quote attributed to George Bernard Shaw: "The greatest problem in communication is the illusion that it has been accomplished."*

2. DO THEY KNOW HOW TO DO IT?

Look at the efforts that people are putting in versus the results they are getting out of those efforts.

There are basic things to address, like knowing how to operate the computer and various other pieces of office equipment. It's important not to overlook these things by assuming that everyone knows how to operate them or that they can figure it out.

There are also industry basics: do they know how to process applications or inventory, and do they know how to ask questions of clients or customers in order to serve them properly?

Ask them things like the following:

- How do you pivot to a cross-sell after taking care of the customer's initial question or concern?
- How do you have a positive conversation with somebody about additional needs or offer other products?

This is all about thinking from a sales *and* service perspective and knowing how to be effective at the work you are asking them to do.

The key is thinking through what you expect from each individual employee throughout his or her entire workday. It really comes down to ensuring their basic knowledge and then helping them *internalize* those concepts and *personalize* them into their own style of doing the work.

3. ARE THEY CONFIDENT IN THEIR ABILITY TO DO IT?

I often hear about *call reluctance*. Sometimes people feel uncomfortable bringing up a certain topic of conversation or pivoting to a different product to see if the customer or prospect has any additional needs. The salesperson might be thinking, "They're probably too busy" or "That's too awkward."

When we don't have confidence in our ability, even if we know *what* to do and know *how* to do it, then

- we're not going to do it,
- we're not going to do it consistently, or
- we're not going to be very effective when we do it.

If you have accountability *systems* set up, and you talk to people each week or month about accomplishing what they committed to, they are going to feel pressure to do it. At the same time, they're not going to be very enthused and excited about it if they don't feel confident in their abilities. That's where coaching can be really useful.

If you can ask sincerely curious open-ended questions, they may feel comfortable enough to say, "Truthfully, I get really nervous when I do this." Or "I don't think I'm good at this." Then you'll open up a great opportunity to provide more training and some personalized coaching to increase their confidence and skill level. Help them remember how they've met similar challenges in the past or how other people have handled the discomfort until they had practiced enough.

You can train people what to do and how to do it, but at some point, confidence just comes from doing it. No matter how much coaching you do with somebody, you can't say anything to make somebody confident. You *can* help them identify what's blocking them from practicing until they get comfortable.

Once they start taking action, act as their cheerleader and encourage them to keep trying. State *your* confidence that they can do it. Their *full* confidence will come from proof that they can do it, which comes from practice. What I've seen is that people become confident when they start having a little success. Even minor successes build on each other. Set the bar low at first, recognize their achievement, and keep moving the bar up. This is called setting them up for success!

4. ARE THEY WILLING TO DO IT?

You can see that the first three areas have to do with training and coaching. When you get to this fourth area of employee performance, it's really about one thing: Is this the right job for them?

Not everybody is a perfect fit for all jobs. If you have someone who knows what they should be doing and how to do it, and it's not about their confidence but more about their willingness to do the work, then you need to ask if the person and the job are the right fit for each other.

As with any relationship, these four key areas of employee performance are about being aware of nuances and listening for clues. Once you've looked at these four areas, then you know what type of conversation to have with your team members and what type of coaching, training, or systems need to be developed to help them be successful.

Your whole goal is to help others be successful. If you help your employees become highly successful, then you all succeed.

CHAPTER 20

Understanding Employee Engagement

Gaining skill as a talent connoisseur is one of the first steps in building a highly engaged sales team, because you are deliberately putting people in the position to succeed by letting them work from their strengths. **Employee engagement is also about building trust and addressing potential obstacles.**

I know I make it sound easier than it is. If you are struggling with this, you are not alone. Remember that Gallup research shows 70% of employees are disengaged from their work, across all industries!

In a Fast Company article discussing Gallup's "State of the American Workforce" report, author Mark C. Crowly described workplace engagement this way:

"To fully comprehend these grim stats, imagine a crew team out on the Potomac River where three people are rowing their hearts out, five are taking in the scenery, and two are trying to sink the boat."

Imagine your business team floating down the river. How many passionate rowers do you

have? How many mostly watch the scenery go by? Do you have any that bring down the office?

WHAT IS EMPLOYEE ENGAGEMENT?

Gallup defines engaged employees as **people who have an emotional connection to the organization they work for and the goals and objectives of that organization.** In other words, they care about the business reaching its goals. Often *that* means more to them than a bonus.

It's also helpful to understand the opposite of employee engagement: active disengagement. Of the 70% of employees who are disengaged, roughly 2 out of 10 are actively disengaged. This means they are unhappy and not productive. These are also the employees likely to spread their dissatisfaction to their coworkers and everyone around them. They may not consciously be trying to "sink the boat," but they do things like the following:

- badmouth the company to friends, family, and coworkers.
- drag down the energy of everyone around them by complaining or by constantly pointing out anything negative.
- take advantage of sick leave policies or steal company resources.

In between the *actively* disengaged and engaged employees are those who are just disengaged. They may be satisfied, but they are not committed to your goals. They're the kind of people you'll find with the "another day, another dollar" attitude. They show up for the paycheck but have no emotional attachment to the results of the organization.

Remember that Gallup estimates the cost to the US economy of disengaged employees is $450–550 billion. Disengaged employees are more likely to

- have chronic illnesses such as diabetes and/or a heart condition, and/or be obese, and/or
- report episodes of depression and other mental illnesses.

Engaged employees are also *far* more likely to be satisfied in life and in their other relationships. Not only is there a huge impact on the productivity of an organization, but being disengaged at work is also very unhealthy for the worker. Since we spend at least 40 hours per week at work, it's valuable to have a strong personal connection to the results we're trying to produce.

WHEN <u>YOU</u> CARE ENOUGH TO CREATE A PROACTIVE, FOCUSED CULTURE, YOU'LL GET EMPLOYEE ENGAGEMENT

At the baseline, you can foster employee engagement by creating a proactive, results-focused culture.

What does this mean? It means that

- Your team is conditioned to focus on income-generating activities.
- Their expectations are clear.
- They aren't simply reacting to stimulus that's coming in (e.g., answering phones, working with customers who come in).
- They approach each task with a +1 attitude. For example, any time an insurance client comes in to make a payment, your team naturally tries to find *one* other thing they can assist that person with, whether it's getting a review scheduled or talking about financing their car with the agency.

It only takes 30–45 seconds to do a +1 activity, but when everybody in the office does that in *every* encounter, it creates a high level of service for the customer. Of course, it also drives results.

I know I've said this already, but I have to stress that clarifying employee expectations is an *essential* first step in creating an engaged team. In fact, it's the first of 12 elements Gallup's research identified as crucial for employee engagement. I'll list the 12 elements here—notice the vast majority of these are within your influence as a leader!

1. I know what is expected of me at work.
2. I have the materials and equipment I need to do my work right.
3. At work, I have the opportunity to do what I do best every day.
4. In the last seven days, I have received recognition or praise for doing good work.

5. My supervisor, or someone at work, seems to care about me as a person.
6. There is someone at work who encourages my development.
7. At work, my opinions seem to count.
8. The mission or purpose of my company makes me feel my job is important.
9. My associates or fellow employees are committed to doing quality work.
10. I have a best friend at work.
11. In the last six months, someone at work has talked to me about my progress.
12. This last year, I have had opportunities at work to learn and grow.

Imagine having an engaged team that is passionate about your business. It's possible. The first step is to measure your team's current engagement with a Q12 Assessment. Gallup makes it simple and affordable ($15 per employee) to assess the level of your team's engagement. Once your team takes the Q12 assessment, you'll have the tools and resources needed to develop strengths-based strategies for creating an engaged team. Visit q12.gallup.com for resources and to access the assessment tool.

CHAPTER 21

Strengths-Based Sales

We all sell. Dan Pink went so far as to name his #1 bestselling book *To Sell Is Human*. All of us are selling our ideas to coworkers and supervisors, travel plans to our significant other, and homework goals to our teenagers! So **don't skip this chapter**, even if you don't think sales is part of your job.

There are two major aspects to consider in the sales process:

1. What prospects need from us in order to make a decision
2. How we can best serve their needs, based on our own strengths

This book is about how we can use our strengths to achieve incredible results in life. However, before I propose a strengths-based approach to sales coaching, I'd be remiss if I didn't reiterate that not everyone is a fit for certain roles. Gallup's research has shown that many people will never be exceptional sales people, just like many of us will never be exceptional managers or exceptional golfers. As we've discussed here, when people take their unique talents and turn them into strengths, they skyrocket to success! Just think again about sports icons: they have gifts that they've honed over many years until they become world class. Yet we know the world is full of people with the dream, who did the work, but didn't make the cut. So although I propose using a strengths-based approach to working with your team members, there is still an element of "fit" for the role.

Again, this means getting the right people on the bus and in the right seat on the bus. This reinforces the importance of developing a rigorous advance selection process. With that said, here's a brief introduction to leveraging your strengths when you're in a sales role.

Think of the very best sales person you know. Do you see them? Chances are they are more motivated than everyone else around them. Why is that? There are several motivating factors, but highly motivated people are usually in a role that feeds their strengths.

Each strength brings us a gift, but each strength has needs as well. I briefly introduced one Gallup strength called WOO (Winning Others Over). When WOO is dominant in a person, they love meeting new people, finding out a bit about them, and building quick relationships. They win people over and quickly develop friends.

I know a salesperson with high WOO who thrived in her sales role. She was a natural networker, as WOOs often are. She loved meeting new people, building her contact lists, having follow-up meetings, and making phone calls. She often exceeded her annual sales quota by more than 150%. Then she received a "promotion" into a marketing role. She was so good at what she did, the company thought they'd use her to help design their overall marketing strategy.

However, her supervisor enjoyed working the external aspects of marketing for the company, which left her stuck in the office, designing flyers, developing product briefs, working on spreadsheets, and living in a silo, only interacting with the salespeople occasionally. Although she was naturally driven by her "Achiever" strength and continued to work hard, she was miserable. It was a daily challenge to muster her full motivation, passion, and energy to work; she just trudged through each day.

What happened to the highly successful and fulfilled employee she once was? The company took someone who thrived on lots of client interaction (on the phone as well as frequent customer visits) and put her in a role where she had zero customer contact and infrequent contact with the sales team. One might say they "robbed her of her WOO." Of course, she still had it, but she didn't have the opportunity to employ it.

Here is another example. A very experienced sales person in an insurance agency was exceptional at selling financial services products. She built deep relationships with clients and was so good at helping them design their life strategy that people really trusted her to help them make good decisions.

Then, during a reorganization of the office, she was put in a front desk position that involved meeting new people as they came in the door. Makes sense, right? *She's so good with people, so why not have her be in an "ambassador"-type position?*

However, WOO was very low for her. She had a different strength—"Relator." People with a strong "Relator" strength build deep connections with people. They tend to have fewer but deeper relationships. For her, talking to 30 new people who walked in the door every day was *exhausting*. She could do it, but her sales results reflected that it was continually challenging for her. After the agent looked at her strengths and asked her what she liked doing best, it became obvious she was hard-wired to work with just a few customers and on more complex issues. He moved her back to her old position.

Think about the *Four Domains of Strengths* I mentioned earlier (Executing, Influencing, Relationship Building, and Strategic Thinking).

Do you have people with strengths in each of the domains so that your team is positioned for success? Remember, individuals are not often well-rounded, but teams **must** be!

As I mentioned earlier, I highly suggest having your team take the Clifton Strengths-Finder® assessment. Take a look at their top five strengths. How can you help them use those strengths at work to fire up their internal motivation?

Do they love to learn? If so, they'll get bored quickly doing the same thing over and over again.

Do they love to think about the future and figure out how to solve future problems? They may excel helping clients plan for retirement.

Not sure? Ask your team members after they've read their strengths report. Go through each of their top five strengths. Ask them what aspect of each particular strength excites them. How might they use that strength every day to increase their fulfillment on the job?

The first key to sales success for your team is to help each of them ensure they are using their strengths throughout the day. It may not be readily apparent to them, but with your coaching and continual practice, they will start to see how using their strengths at work will help them love their job. It will also heighten their engagement in achieving the results you're looking for: a true win-win.

BUILDING YOUR TEAM

Another aspect of successful sales is thinking through *how* the work gets done. Face it: there are parts of any role that are a bit of a "grind." For example, there are reports to analyze, new information to absorb, prospects to find and nurture, forms to be completed, regulations and rules to follow, applications to fill out, and numerous follow-up activities. Whew—exhausting! That doesn't even consider the many different products to understand!

Helping team members learn how to use their strengths to ensure success with these pre- and postsales activities is crucial. Some of the best sales people I know are not that great at follow-up, but clients demand exceptional follow-up—a bit of a dilemma. Build continual strengths coaching sessions into your regular routine with each team member.

For team members who don't have *organizational or focus* strengths, ask them how they can use the strengths they do have to ensure critical details aren't missed.

Sometimes this will involve helping them build systems, checklists, and routines into their day. Other times, it may be best for them to partner with another person on the team. If someone is exceptional at discovery conversations, building trust, solving needs, and helping clients make decisions that result in sales, but not so great at the detail work, find someone on the team to help them be organized and follow through.

Chances are, you can drive increased sales by partnering team members who have complementary strengths—in other words, team members who have strengths where others have weaknesses.

So far, we've talked about motivation and creating strengths-based sales systems. Now let's talk about clients.

How do your team members build relationships, ask good questions, decide which of your solutions would be most helpful to clients, present those solutions in a compelling way, and motivate clients to make decisions?

What motivates them to pivot to a needed product discussion and how can they be most effective in that pivot?

SALES PROCESS/SYSTEM

How can you train and coach your team so their sales efforts are not just a transaction but also a truly fruitful needs-based discussion? Gallup's research shows that *highly successful sales people don't sell the same way*! There are many different sales systems. The 34 strengths influence <u>how</u> an individual salesperson could approach each sales system and still see success.

That's one of the problems with most sales trainings. They teach that one particular trainer's sales system is the best system for all. The idea that any one sales system, <u>done one particular way</u> by all sales people is best, is wrong. Yes, some sales systems are better than others. You'll see many commonalities among people, but remember, the chances of any two salespeople having the same top five strengths are 1 in 33 million! Gallup's research shows that the most successful salespeople have developed their own sales approach by combining their unique talents with their knowledge, professional sales skills, and practice. Notice that knowledge and skills can be developed through training—talent cannot. The question is *How do you help your sales people bring out their best?*

Your best approach is to think about what each client needs during the sales process, finalize the sales system that you want to standardize with, then coach team members *individually* to help them learn how to use their strengths to be successful using that system.

I'll touch on a few examples, but the most effective process will be to help your team members customize their approach to different aspects of the sales process, depending on their strengths.

PROSPECTING

Do your team members talk to people in the coffee line and encourage these new contacts to come by for a quote/a visit?

Does someone on your team have fewer close relationships but tend to bring in a lot of family and friends who become clients? That will be their strengths at play. Some team members high in "Relationship" strengths may approach others wherever they find them.

What if you have a team member who is high in the "Strategic" strength? They may get excited about being in charge of your booth at tradeshows or conferences. Let your WOOs walk around talking about your business during the show. Find someone else, back at the office, who is great at following up personally with the business cards/raffle entries your WOOs gathered and who can be relied on to get those new contacts into your keep-in-touch marketing system (like a newsletter). This might be someone who is high in "Discipline or Responsibility."

I worked with one office that had two team members who loved cold calling! They were high in competition and loved picking up the phone and calling person after person looking for that win. People with different strengths will naturally take a different approach to helping your build your business.

Also, look at those who actually provide your service or product. Do they know how to ask for referrals in a natural way, immediately after they have provided an exceptional experience to your clients?

BUILDING RAPPORT AND THEN BUILDING A *TRUSTED ADVISOR* RELATIONSHIP

Ask each team member how he or she builds friendships or how he or she might go about it. Look at team members' strengths reports and help them determine the best way to go about building rapport with prospects. How can they consciously utilize their skills/knowledge/experience and strengths to build relationships with prospects and clients so that they come to be viewed as that person's *trusted advisor* in your industry. Again, help them do this consciously and help them understand that being a *trusted advisor* is their goal.

MONEY, AUTHORITY, NEED

1. Have you helped each of your sales people find a natural, comfortable way to ask the customer for their budget or what they were looking to spend? That must be done before proposing a solution, or your team is likely wasting time.

2. Are they talking to the actual decision maker? It should be easy for them to ask, "Who else will be involved in making the decision? Who will be the final decision maker?" Make sure your team *always* asks these questions *early* in the process so that they don't have to repeat themselves or risk being misquoted as their contact is trying to sell your solution up the authority chain.

3. Many people use the terms "discovery questions" or "fact-finding" to describe the *needs* part of the sales process. By now, you're getting the

idea that this will mean different things to different people. Someone high in "Learner," "Input," or "Relator" strengths may be genuinely interested in discovering something new about others. How will others on your team who don't naturally approach life from a "Learner" or "Input" perspective handle this process? Experiment a bit—ask your team members how they would use their own natural strengths to be effective in discovering the specific underlying needs of your prospects. Help them develop their curiosity in a way that feeds their own needs while effectively uncovering all the needs of the client—even those needs the client doesn't see or want to admit.

If the client hasn't mentioned a need that you are typically able to fulfill, does your team member have a method of pivoting to that topic that suits their natural strengths? Do you require that each sales person ask questions in each of the areas that your products and services serve? Make sure each salesperson is comfortable pivoting a discussion about one area to another and then another so that each discovery session is thorough and a good use of your salesperson and the client's time.

CLARIFYING CONSEQUENCES

The best salespeople are really good at asking "What will happen if you don't solve that issue?" when a prospect brings up a concern or need. Prospects won't normally volunteer this information, so the salesperson needs to be comfortable being very direct and assertive during this portion of the sales process. *You have to quantify the risks* to the prospect of not acting on the problem. The more detail, and the more consequences that the salesperson can uncover, the more likely you are to provide a very valuable service.

GAINING AGREEMENT

After the salesperson uncovers all the prospect's current pain and potential specific risks (as well as their budget and authority), it should be easy to gain agreement from the client that *if* the solution fulfills the need or solves the problem, they will take action (like signing your contract or subscribing to your service).

It is worth summarizing all these points and then asking if they have any other concerns. Ask them what the decision-making process will be. If they're not clear about that, the salesperson must be willing to help the client get clear about the process. Once both are clear on the process, the salesperson needs to ask the direct question, "Okay, assuming that our proposed solution meets the need or solves this problem and is within your budget, do you agree that there would be no reason not to move forward with us?" You need to know if they're just shopping for a third price to satisfy some checklist somewhere. There's nothing that says you have to go to the time and trouble of proposing a solution.

If the sale is very complex, have the salesperson come to you at this point and decide if you're going to proceed to the proposal development stage or just thank the prospect for his or her time. You've *got* to be efficient with your team's time in order to be successful!

IDENTIFYING AND CUSTOMIZING SOLUTIONS

Remember, "A confused mind never buys." Whoever is responsible for developing solutions needs to have enough information to select one to three solutions and then work with the salesperson to make sure they cover all the prospect's needs. Make sure the salesperson understands all the features and benefits, so they can match them to each pain or risk. Have the salesperson write the proposal, matching their personality and the customer's language/sophistication level (and guess the customer's top strengths if you don't know them). Make sure you consider whether the prospect is tactile, visual, or auditory too.

OBJECTIONS

Make sure your salespeople are good at anticipating and overcoming objections. This is best done in team meetings. Their learning will be aided by having you and product experts present. Have your salespeople record all the objections they get and create a FAQ for the rest of your sales team and for future sales team members. Again, consider how people with different strengths can best handle these objections and consider whether the prospect will want a lot of data to answer their concern or a testimonial from a previous/existing client.

NEGOTIATING AND CLOSING

Role play and practice this all the time, initially privately, and then in your team meetings. Each strength can be used differently, but the objective is always for each salesperson to be very comfortable with what they can and cannot negotiate and asking for the sale. Even your "Input" people should be comfortable with a question like "Okay, what would you like me to do now?" They've got to ask for the signature and then cocreate a plan for the next steps with their new client. Explain to your salespeople that they are responsible for holding the client's hand through the process.

FULFILLMENT PROCESS

Next comes the fulfillment process, whatever that is for your business. Make *sure* that the salesperson double checks the start of this process to make ensure it is going to create the solution that they promised the client.

FOLLOW-UP/NURTURING/CROSS-SELLING/UPSELLING

Always be sure there is guaranteed follow-up after the sale and continue to keep in touch with your clients. A person who is high in the strength, "Responsibility" is a good one to oversee this process. Make sure your new client knows who to contact and how to contact that person, and do so by verbalizing expectations, so everyone is on the same page. Make sure the salesperson checks the first bill before it goes out. By doing all these things, you have the best chance of cross-selling, upselling, and getting testimonials and referrals from the new client.

TRAINING YOUR TEAM

True strengths are made up of three components: knowledge, skills, and talent. Of course we need to understand the product we are selling and be skilled at delivering the message, but we're also most effective if we use natural talents to develop our own unique approach to the sales process.

Knowledge is what we know. Skill is what we can do. Talents are those naturally reoccurring patterns of thoughts, feelings, and actions. Your training program needs to consider all three of these components.

Oftentimes, training stops at delivering knowledge. You may have an operations manual or online training program that's designed to deliver the knowledge needed to sell your product. However, that's only the first step. To develop skills—the ability to do something—you must incorporate practice and effective feedback. People learn best from their own experiences. You can help team members make sense out of their own experiences by encouraging early application of the new knowledge, then ask questions that help them understand what went well, what they learned, and what they will change next time. Remember, you can use Gallup's Clifton StrengthsFinder® to identify natural talent in each team member. Then start discussing how your team member will incorporate their natural talents into the sales process.

Strengths even come into play when considering how to train your team! When you're thinking about designing your training program, consider different modes of delivery. Of course your team needs company, product, compliance, licensing, and sales training.

We all need more good ideas and guidance on how we can best implement those ideas. *However, what areas can you customize based on the strengths of each team member?*

For instance, team members that have high "Learner" or "Input" may benefit from sitting in front of the computer and taking online modules. A team member who worked for a successful insurance agent once told me, "I really enjoyed studying for my insurance exams. It was so interesting!"

However, a team member with "Activator" would probably prefer being out in the field where the action is. The key is to think through what type of training is most effective for each team member.

A six-week or six-month training program will not develop excellence in anyone. If you really want exceptionally talented team members who differentiate your business from the business down the street, you need a continual commitment to a multifaceted training program that not only incorporates new knowledge but also helps your team learn from their own experiences.

CHAPTER 22

Why Building Trust Is Essential for Highly Engaged Teams

We've talked about how meetings can help your team stay on task, but in order for that to work, you must have open communication. It's essential for you to identify key activities that drive results *and* be able to speak comfortably and candidly about the successes, mental blocks, and other challenges people face in doing those activities. At the foundation, **this is about building trust among team members**.

Patrick Lencioni identified common elements that keep teams from operating at their best in his best-selling book *The Five Dysfunctions of a Team*. (If you don't already have that book, it belongs on your bookshelf along with his follow-up book *Overcoming the Five Dysfunctions of a Team*.)

Those five elements are as follows:

1. Absence of trust
2. Fear of conflict
3. Lack of commitment
4. Avoidance of accountability
5. Inattention to results

1. ABSENCE OF TRUST

The foundational level to work on for creating a highly engaged team is building trust. It's up to you, as the leader, to foster trust within your organization. Gallup's book *Strengths Based Leadership* also emphasizes trust as a key element to success. Every team has four basic needs: trust, compassion, stability, and hope. This is as much about trust between team members and their leader as it is about trust between team members.

How Do We Build Trust?

Willingness to be vulnerable is central to building trust. As a leader, this can be difficult to embrace because we've all been told that being 100% honest and open will result in being hurt or not respected. In reality, the opposite is true. This is a key element of taking a strengths-based approach to leadership.

As leaders, we need to do the following:

1. Understand our strengths and leverage them
2. Understand, admit to, and accept our weaknesses
3. Be transparent about our fears and concerns and invite people to understand where we're coming from
4. Ask our team members to fill in those areas of weakness for us

But modeling vulnerability is just the beginning. You must also find ways to help your team members be transparent, accept their weaknesses, and be open about their fears. In the absence of trust, people not only hide their weaknesses, fears, and mistakes from one another but also are hesitant to ask for or offer help. In the absence of trust, we end up working in an office of silos, with people overlapping work and huge gaps that no one notices.

Avoid the Blame Game

One way to foster trust among team members is to implement after-action reviews (AAR). One of my great mentors, Larry Broughton, took this concept from his time in the Special Forces and applied it to his hotel chain. After every event, his team would convene and talk about how it went, what was challenging, and what was done well. It was not about pointing fingers at each other if something went wrong. That doesn't mean that you shouldn't take responsibility, but no one can change the past. An AAR is not about personalities; it focuses on identifying how to move forward as a team—that is, how to make sure next time is better. What procedures can you put in place that will guarantee success to the highest extent possible? During an AAR, the leader asks three questions:

1. What happened?
2. What did we learn?
3. How can we do it differently in the future? (For example, how can we build in double checks and fail safes? Or, how can we do it even better?)

Highly engaged teams are those that see each member as a whole person, with strengths and weaknesses. **We're all in a learning process, all the time. When people are recognized in such a way, they are more willing to see others the same way.** They're more willing to work together from a place of trust that elevates the entire team. Sounds good, doesn't it? It is!

When you shift your focus away from blame, even if someone did drop the ball, the team will be too engaged in the solution and the idea of doing it better in the future to have negative, self-defeating conversations.

CHAPTER 23

Four Obstacles to a Truly Engaged Team

In order to create a highly engaged team, you must recognize and address common obstacles to getting there. You know that trust is a top priority when building your team. But what's next?

We've already looked at the first obstacle identified in the *Five Dysfunctions of a Team*. Let's look at the next four obstacles that can prevent you from getting to the next level.

2. FEAR OF CONFLICT

It's probably safe to say that most of us have a fear of conflict. How do you know if it's alive in your team? If your meetings are pretty boring, this is probably true. If people just go along with whatever you say, then go back to work and don't actually implement the strategies discussed, *you* may have a fear of conflict. If the team isn't engaging in a back-and-forth dialogue with you, most likely it's because *they* don't want to rock the boat. They probably don't feel safe expressing their opinions. This also means they haven't bought in to what you are trying to accomplish. This is when you need to make sure you are doing things to foster trust (make it safe to disagree) and help people leverage their individual strengths.

What you are looking for is commitment or buy-in from each team member. This means that you have set clear expectations and have a system of accountability in place. It also means that **you *want* pushback from your team if they feel your expectations are not reasonable**. If you have enough trust, they should be able to comfortably tell you that they have too much on their plate and need to adjust their workload. Members of an engaged team won't be worried about their leader or teammates perceiving such a request as weakness.

Mine for Conflict to Create a More Highly Engaged Team

One way to help alleviate the possibility of conflict, or the fear of it, is by recognizing where it might arise and being proactive about it. This means that if your team members have committed to certain tasks, as the leader, you should then ask them if they are comfortable with performing those tasks *and* the size of their workload. Reiterating that they are making a commitment to accomplishing certain things gives them the opportunity to avoid overcommitting and the subsequent stress that comes with not feeling successful. It also gives them the chance to address any concerns.

3. LACK OF COMMITMENT

A lack of trust and a fear of conflict lead to a lack of commitment. Sometimes people are too focused on "watching their back"; they're afraid of getting slammed for making a mistake. We can't fully commit when we don't feel safe saying what we really think. It's that simple. That's why mining for conflict is so important. If you've asked for open expression of conflict and built trust, people are then free to truly commit. An engaged team reflects that kind of freedom.

Be Specific

Perhaps you got their buy-in, but you aren't seeing results. That may be because you were too vague about the commitment. This is where your objectives come in. If you agree to start increasing phone calls throughout the week, that's all well and good, but where are we now? Increase by how exactly? How many? When do we start? When you attach metrics to commitments, then people really know what they're committing to and they can talk about what is realistic for them. Remember, **when expectations are crystal clear, it's easy to move forward.**

4. AVOIDANCE OF ACCOUNTABILITY

A committed team makes it easier to hold each other accountable. When you have members of your team who avoid accountability, it can result in resentment from other team members and encourage mediocrity throughout the team. That's why *it is crucial to hold all team members equally accountable.* Remember that Gallup's Q12 research revealed 12 areas that create highly engaged teams. One of the areas reflects this notion of accountability: *"My fellow employees are committed to doing quality work."*

They found that when some people on the team are not committed to doing their best, it brings down the productivity of the entire team.

How do you know that your team is not avoiding accountability? They are excited about what they commit to and eager to help each other out. Everyone is held to the same high standard of performance and you're all in it together.

5. INATTENTION TO RESULTS

With this foundation of trust, transparency, commitment, and accountability, you should be able to be open about your results. If your team does not know how they are held accountable and you do not share results, that foundation is eroded. With a highly engaged team, you can build excitement about your results—and even healthy competition. Think about how our culture rallies around sports: the excitement is contagious when points are scored.

If your team is invested in the result—if they've bought into the commitment—they are going to rally around the results. It's a remarkable thing to see. When you arrive at this place, you know that you have built an engaged team that can overcome any obstacle.

Conclusion

We've covered a lot of ground. Hopefully these concepts and resources will serve you well for years to come. However, it's been my experience that a lot of people, myself included, read a book or go to a seminar and never implement any of the ideas they once were excited about. So my suggestion is to start with the following three areas:

1. **Your Strengths:** Take your full 34 strengths assessment and start to consider how you can use your natural strengths to build an exceptional business and how you can best manage around the things at the bottom of your list.
2. **Team Strengths:** Have your team members take the assessment to get their top five strengths. Share all the results with the entire team and plan regular meetings to talk about each person's unique strengths. Gallup suggests developing strengths using the terms "Name," "Claim," and "Aim." First off, help team members become familiar with the terminology and the descriptions of each theme. Then ask them to share how these strengths themes have shown up in their lives. Finally, help them start to develop strengths-based strategies to aim their unique talents toward the results you jointly identify.
3. **Engagement:** Strengths, of course, tie into engagement. Have your team take the Q12 assessment and conduct debriefs shortly thereafter to identify an engagement element for you and/or the team to focus on. Consider employee engagement *Job #1*! When reviewing your assessment results, begin by focusing on the first elements of engagement. Starting with #1 (*I know what is expected of me at work*) is a great place to start.

Finally, you can't do this alone. None of us can. It's not only challenging to think through how to apply these ideas to our businesses but also hard to hold ourselves accountable for doing what we know we should do! Here are several ideas for internalizing, expanding, and implementing these best practices.

FREE

- Establish accountability partnerships with a friend who is also on a growth path. It's helpful if they are slightly ahead of you or at least at the same level. However, you can develop accountability partnerships with anyone who is committed to the process.
- Start a structured mastermind/study group. Organize a group to meet regularly for each person to share their goals, challenges, and opportunities. The rest of the mastermind can give feedback and help hold each person accountable for completing the tasks they agree on.
- Find a highly successful peer and ask them to mentor you for a while. It's a small investment to buy lunch for someone whom you admire and who is farther down the path. It's also a powerful experience to serve as a mentor for newer business leaders. Just thinking through how you will help them will help you stay focused on your own key business metrics and actions.

INVESTMENT

- Develop a continual personal-renewal program. Buy a copy of *Flashpoints for Achievers* by Larry Broughton. This book is full of inspiring messages and wisdom from an award-winning CEO. Spend a little time each day reflecting on the messages and thinking of how you can make continual slight improvements in your life and business.
- Hire a coach. In an interview for *Fortune* magazine's "The Best Advice I Ever Got" video, Google CEO Eric Schmidt states, "Everybody needs a coach." We all need others who have our best interests at heart, yet will help us see ourselves as we really are. Coaches give people perspective and help them see the impact their actions (or inactions) may be having on others. A professionally trained coach is highly skilled at helping people discover and remove mental blocks and tap into their own resources to move forward.
- There are a variety of mastermind groups offered for a fee. If this is of interest, I suggest doing through research online and then seeing if you can talk to a few people who have experienced the group.

There are, of course, a million and a half things we could do with our time. I'm grateful you spent some of your time with me. I believe there's no higher calling than helping others succeed. That's how I see the role of a business leader—helping their team members flourish. What a legacy to have multiple people who can point back to you as the person who helped them learn how to light their own fire—to become exceptional.

Best wishes in your pursuit of an exceptional business with an exceptional team.

To your success!

Keith Baldwin, M. Ed., CPC

Book Resources

The following materials are available for download through the "Resource" tab at www.keithbaldwin.com. I encourage you to print these for your planning and execution strategies.

Personal Reinvention Guide

Business Success Wheel

90-Day Game Plan Template

Values Exercise

SWOT Analysis Template

Bibliography

Adkins, Amy. "Only 35% of U.S. Managers Are Engaged in Their Jobs." *Gallup*, April 2, 2015. Accessed April 26, 2015. http://www.gallup.com/businessjournal/182228/managers-engaged-jobs.aspx.

Broughton, Larry. "Flashpoints for Achievers." Yoogozi Motivation Inspiration Leadership, June 30, 2014. Accessed April 26, 2015. http://yoogozi.com/flashpoints.

———. *Flashpoints for Achievers: Inspiring Messages That Bring Significant Results; A Daily Journal.* Pro App Creators, LLC, 2014.

Buckingham, Marcus, and Curt Coffman. *First, Break All the Rules: What the World's Greatest Managers Do Differently.* New York: Simon and Schuster, 1999.

Calhoon, Joe. *The One Hour Plan for Growth: How a Single Sheet of Paper Can Take Your Business to the Next Level.* Hoboken, NJ: John Wiley, 2011.

Clifton StrengthsFinder® THEMES. *Gallup.* Accessed April 26, 2015. http://www.gallup.com/file/poll/166991/Strengths_QuickRefCard_en-US_0712v3_bk.pdf.

Coffman, Curt. "The High Cost of Disengaged Employees." *Gallup*, April 15, 2002. Accessed April 26, 2015. http://www.gallup.com/businessjournal/247/the-high-cost-of-disengaged-employees.aspx.

Coffman, Curt, and Gabriel González Molina. *Follow This Path: How the World's Greatest Organizations Drive Growth by Unleashing Human Potential.* New York: Warner, 2002.

Collins, James, and Jerry Porras. "Building Your Company's Vision." *Harvard Business Review*, September 1, 1996. Accessed April 26, 2015. https://hbr.org/1996/09/building-your-companys-vision.

Collins, Jim. "Good to Great." *Jimcollins.com*, October 2001. Accessed April 26, 2015. http://www.jimcollins.com/article_topics/articles/good-to-great.html.

———. *Good to Great: Why Some Companies Make the Leap . . . and Others Don't.* New York: Harper, 2001.

Coonradt, Charles A., and Lee Nelson. *The Game of Work.* Layton, UT: Gibbs Smith, 2012.

Crowley, Mark C. "Gallup's Workplace Jedi on How to Fix Our Employee Engagement Problem." *Fast Company*, June 4, 2013. Accessed April 26, 2015. http://www.fastcompany.com/3011032/creative-conversations/gallups-workplace-jedi-on-how-to-fix-our-employee-engagement-problem.

"Customer Engagement." *Customer Engagement.* Accessed April 26, 2015. http://www.gallup.com/topic/customer_engagement.aspx.

Daloz, Laurent A. *Mentor: Guiding the Journey of Adult Learners.* San Francisco: Jossey-Bass, 1999.

Deci, Edward L., and Richard Flaste. *Why We Do What We Do: Understanding Self-Motivation*. New York: Penguin, 1996.

"Five Dysfunctions Resources." *The Five Dysfunctions of a Team*. Accessed April 26, 2015. http://www.tablegroup.com/books/dysfunctions.

Gallup. "Gallup Employee Engagement Center." *Gallup Q12 Employee Engagement Center*. Accessed April 26, 2015. http://q12.gallup.com.

———. "Gallup Strengths Center." *YouTube*. Accessed April 26, 2015. http://www.youtube.com/user/GallupStrengths.

———. "Gallup Strengths Center." *Strengths Coaches' Playbook: Called to Coach Recap; Keith Baldwin*, August 8, 2014. Accessed April 26, 2015. http://coaching.gallup.com/2014/08/called-to-coach-recap-keith-baldwin-aug.html.

———. "Report: State of the American Workplace." *Gallup*. Accessed April 26, 2015. http://www.gallup.com/services/176708/state-american-workplace.aspx.

Harter, Jim. "Mondays Not So 'Blue' for Engaged Employees." *Gallup*, July 23, 2012. Accessed April 26, 2015. http://www.gallup.com/poll/155924/Mondays-Not-Blue-Engaged-Employees.aspx.

Harter, Jim, and Amy Adkins. "Employees Want a Lot More from Their Managers." *Gallup*, April 8, 2015. Accessed April 26, 2015. http://www.gallup.com/businessjournal/182321/employees-lot-managers.aspx.

Harter, Jim, and Sangeeta Agrawal. "Actively Disengaged Workers and Jobless in Equally Poor Health." *Gallup*, April 20, 2011. Accessed April 26, 2015. http://www.gallup.com/poll/147191/Actively-Disengaged-Workers-Jobless-Equally-Poor-Health.aspx.

Heskett, James L., Earl W. Sasser, and Joe Wheeler. *The Ownership Quotient: Putting the Service Profit Chain to Work for Unbeatable Competitive Advantage*. Boston: Harvard Business Press, 2008.

ICF Coaching FAQs. Accessed April 27, 2015. http://coachfederation.org/about/landing.cfm?ItemNumber=844&navItemNumber=617.

Lencioni, Patrick. *Death by Meeting: A Leadership Fable about Solving the Most Painful Problem in Business*. San Francisco: Jossey-Bass, 2004.

———. *The Five Dysfunctions of a Team: A Leadership Fable*. San Francisco: Jossey-Bass, 2002.

McChesney, Chris, Sean Covey, and Jim Huling. *The 4 Disciplines of Execution: Achieving Your Wildly Important Goals*. New York: Free Press, 2012.

Pink, Daniel H. *Drive: The Surprising Truth about What Motivates Us*. New York: Riverhead, 2009.

———. "RSA Animate—Drive: The Surprising Truth about What Motivates Us." *YouTube*, April 1, 2010. Accessed April 26, 2015. https://www.youtube.com/watch?v=u6XAPnuFjJc.

———. *To Sell Is Human: The Surprising Truth about Moving Others*. New York: Riverhead, 2012.

Rath, Tom. *Strengths Finder 2.0*. New York: Gallup, 2007.

Rath, Tom, and Barry Conchie. *Strengths Based Leadership: Great Leaders, Teams, and Why People Follow*. New York: Gallup, 2008.

———. "What Followers Want from Leaders." *Gallup*, January 8, 2009. Accessed April 26, 2015. http://www.gallup.com/businessjournal/113542/what-followers -want-from-leaders.aspx.

———. "What Makes a Great Leadership Team?" *Gallup*, February 3, 2009. Accessed April 26, 2015. http://www.gallup.com/businessjournal/113338/what-makes -great-leadership-team.aspx.

Rutigliano, Tony, and Brian Brim. *Strengths Based Selling: Based on Decades of Gallup's Research into High-performing Salespeople*. New York: Gallup, 2010.

Smith, Benson, and Tony Rutigliano. *Discover Your Sales Strengths: How the World's Greatest Salespeople Develop Winning Careers*. New York: Warner, 2003.

Sorenson, Susan. "Lower Your Health Costs While Boosting Performance." *Gallup*, September 19, 2013. Accessed April 26, 2015. http://www.gallup.com/ businessjournal/164420/lower-health-costs-boosting-performance.aspx.

Sorenson, Susan, and Keri Garman. "How to Tackle U.S. Employees' Stagnating Engagement." *Gallup*, June 11, 2013. Accessed April 26, 2015. http://www.gallup .com/businessjournal/162953/tackle-employees-stagnating-engagement.aspx.

Wagner, Rodd, and James K. Harter. *12: The Elements of Great Managing*. New York: Gallup, 2006.